Match of My Life

WIGAN WARRIORS

KNOW THE SCORE BOOKS PUBLICATIONS

CULT HEROES	Author	ISBN
CHELSEA	Leo Moynihan	1-905449-00-3
MANCHESTER CITY	David Clayton	978-1-905449-05-7
NEWCASTLE	Dylan Younger	1-905449-03-8
SOUTHAMPTON	Jeremy Wilson	1-905449-01-1
WEST BROM	Simon Wright	1-905449-02-X

MATCH OF MY LIFE	Editor	ISBN
ENGLAND WORLD CUP	Massarella & Moynihan	1-905449-52-6
EUROPEAN CUP FINALS	Ben Lyttleton	1-905449-57-7
FA CUP FINALS	David Saffer	978-1-905449-53-8
FULHAM	Michael Heatley	1-905449-51-8
LEEDS	David Saffer	1-905449-54-2
LIVERPOOL	Leo Moynihan	1-905449-50-X
SHEFFIELD UNITED	Nick Johnson	1-905449-62-3
STOKE CITY	Simon Lowe	978-1-905449-55-2
SUNDERLAND	Rob Mason	1-905449-60-7
SPURS	Allen & Massarella	978-1-905449-58-3
WOLVES	Simon Lowe	1-905449-56-9

GENERAL FOOTBALL	Author	ISBN
WORLD CUP DIARY	Harry Harris	1-905449-90-9
HOLD THE BACK PAGE	Harry Harris	1-905449-91-7

AUTOBIOGRAPHY	Author	ISBN
TACKLES LIKE A FERRET (England Cover)	Paul Parker	1-905449-47-X
TACKLES LIKE A FERRET (Manchester United Cover)	Paul Parker	1-905449-46-1

FOOTBALL FICTION	Author	ISBN
BURKSEY The Autobiography of a Football God	Peter Morfoot	1-905449-49-6

RUGBY LEAGUE	Author	ISBN
WIGAN WARRIORS	David Kuzio	978-1905449-66-8

CRICKET	Author	ISBN
ASHES TO DUST	Graham Cookson	978-1-905449-19-4
MOML: THE ASHES	Pilger & Wightman	1-905449-63-1
GROVEL!	David Tossell	978-1-905449-43-9
The 1976 West IndiesTour of England		
MY TURN TO SPIN	Shaun Udal	978-1-905449-42-2
WASTED?	Paul Smith	978-1-905449-45-3
LEAGUE CRICKET YEARBOOK	Andy Searle	978-1-905449-70-5
North West edition		
LEAGUE CRICKET YEARBOOK	Andy Searle	978-1-905449-72-9
Midlands edition		

FORTHCOMING PUBLICATIONS IN 2007

CULT HEROES	Author	ISBN
CARLISLE	Paul Harrison	978-1-905449-09-7
CELTIC	David Potter	978-1-905449-08-8
NOTINGHAM FOREST	David McVay	978-1-905449-06-4
RANGERS	Paul Smith	978-1-905449-07-1

MATCH OF MY LIFE	Editor	ISBN
ASTON VILLA	Neil Moxley	978-1-905449-65-1
BOLTON WANDERERS	David Saffer	978-1-905449-64-4
DERBY COUNTY	Johnson & Matthews	978-1-905449-68-2
MANCHESTER UNITED	Ivan Ponting	978-1-905449-59-0

GENERAL FOOTBALL	Author	ISBN
CHAMPIONS LEAGUE YEARBOOK	Harry Harris	978-1-905449-93-4
OUTCASTS	Steve Menary	978-1-905449-31-6
The Lands That FIFA Forgot		
PARISH TO PLANET	Eric Midwinter	978-1-905449-30-9
A History of Football		
MY PREMIERSHIP DIARY	Marcus Hahnemann	978-1-905449-33-0
Reading's Season in the Premiership		

Match of My Life

WIGAN WARRIORS

Editor: David Kuzio

Series Editor: Simon Lowe
Know The Score Books Limited

www.knowthescorebooks.com

First published in the United Kingdom
by Know The Score Books Limited, 2007

Know The Score Books Limited
118 Alcester Road
Studley
Warwickshire
B80 7NT

www.knowthescorebooks.com

A CIP catalogue record is available for this book from the British Library

ISBN-13: 978-1-905449-66-8

Jacket and book design by Lisa David

Printed and bound in Great Britain
By William Clowes UK Ltd, Beccles, Norfolk

Photographs in this book are reproduced by kind permission of:
Colorsport, EMPICS, Kath Nield and Andrew Varley

Front cover:
Top left Ellery Hanley lifts the Challenge Cup into the Wembley
sky after Wigan's victory over Warrington in 1990
Bottom left Billy Boston dodges a Hunslet tackler during a
typically rampaging run in the 1965 Challenge Cup final
Bottom right Shaun Edwards can't hide his glee at winning the
1985 Challenge Cup for his hometown club

Rear cover:
Top left Brian Carney, David Furner, Adrian Lam and Brett Dallas
rejoice with the 2002 Challenge Cup, Wigan's most recent trophy
Top right Terry O'Connor surges past the Halifax defence in
typically barnstorming fashion
Bottom Shaun Edwards and Martin Offiah celebrate Wigan's 1995
Challenge Cup victory over Leeds

Contents

This book is dedicated to my son

Ryan Adam

and my late daughter Kate

– I love you with all my heart.

Editor's Acknowledgements

I WOULD like to thank Simon Lowe, the Managing Director of *Know the Score Books*, first and foremost because if he had not taken my first e-mail seriously and had decided not to risk the reputation of the company on a rugby league book then this idea would still be a pipedream. Thank you Simon for your faith and all your help during this project.

My family have been very supportive, especially my dad Adam, my mum Kathleen and my sister Karen, who along with my fiancée Christine and mother-in-law-to-be Margaret have had to put up with my mood swings and temper tantrums when things were not going too well. In fact Christine was a godsend near the end with her help and support when the deadline was approaching and my health was getting the better of me. My son Ryan has also helped by telling me off when I have been watching television instead of writing my book. It has been difficult and a challenge, but together we got through it.

Graham Emmerson, the Wigan RLFC press officer, was very helpful when it came to tracking down players and the club itself have been very supportive in this project. I would also like to thank Keith Mills for his help with the foreword. Keith has been a loyal servant to the club in many different roles and it is very fitting that he agreed to be involved. Praise also must go out to Mick Hannan, Debbie Ward, Andrew Rimmer (Bilko) and Peter Carroll, who all played their own little parts in making this book complete.

I must offer a big thank you to every player who has been involved in the project. Their co-operation and patience has been fantastic and for all of you I hope your favourite memories come across in the way that you intended. Thank you all so very much.

Finally, I would like to take this opportunity to pay my respects to a man who is no longer with us. Joe Hughes died in April 2007. Joe was the father of one of my best mates Dave Hughes. Joe was a fantastic fellow and loved by a lot of people. He took the time and effort to show an interest in what his son's friends were up to – every time he saw me he would ask how my writing was going – and with him being a big rugby fan I know he would have enjoyed this book. Rest in Peace Joe, you will be missed.

David Kuzio
May 2007

Introduction

WIGAN RUGBY League Club means a lot of things to different people. To me, family aside, Wigan rugby league club is my life. It's the same for thousands of others who have cherry and white in their blood. To others they are despised, hated and some cannot bear to even spell the word out in full, either referring to W**an, or even Wigoon – but this book brings together all the reasons why Wigan rugby league club are known worldwide as one of the greatest clubs in the sport. If you are not a fan of Wigan or do not like reminiscing about the good old days, I think it is time to put the book down.

As I have said, Wigan is my life and before sealing a deal to write this book I was already in the planning stage of writing a book based on the club's eight successive Challenge Cup victories between 1988 until 1995, but one night after a quick search on the internet my subject matter changed. I was ploughing through a number of book sites trying to get inspiration on how to start my next masterpiece, but having no luck until I typed the words "Sheffield United" into Google. To my surprise a book called 'Sheffield United – Match Of My Life' came up along with quite a few more under the publisher *Know the Score Books*.

I decided to email them to see if they had considered ever publishing a series of books based on rugby league clubs in the same format as their footballing ones. To my surprise and delight I received a response from their managing director Simon Lowe asking me to give him a call to discuss matters. Minutes later I was on the phone to Simon putting forward my idea; Simon was very helpful and supportive and admitted this kind of publication would only work with a handful of rugby league clubs, with Wigan being one of them. After a little chat I revealed I had already been in touch with Shaun Edwards, Shaun Wane and Andy Gregory for my earlier idea and we agreed that I should start to compile a list of players I wanted to include and who I thought would have decent tales to tell.

That is where my problems started – how do you compile a list of 14 former Wigan players without them all choosing the same game, or with a decent gap between eras, without alienating older and younger fans. I know people will look at the list of players and say "why did you chose so-and-so" and "He would have been better that him", but it is not as easy as picking up the former Wigan rugby league players' phone book and ordering them like a takeaway. Some players do not want to be found and some do not have very good tales to tell; my job was to find people who would be interesting.

So I knew I already had three 'dead certs' willing to help me – now for the other 11. I only started watching rugby league in 1986, but I have a decent enough history of the club in my mind to know the players of yesteryear who my mum and dad followed as youngsters. Compiling a list of players was very easy – Billy Boston, Joe Egan, Bill Ashurst and Colin Clarke – the hard part was getting in touch with these legends and seeing if they were willing to take part. And, without being too disrespectful, if they could remember the finer details this project needed.

From any Wigan fan's memory you can list plenty of players from the last 20 years who are ideal for this exercise – Ellery Hanley, Joe Lydon, Andrew Farrell, Kris Radlinski, Denis Betts, Colin Clarke, Phil Clarke, Eric Ashton, Martin Offiah and Jason Robinson – all who never made it in the book. Perhaps that means there's romm for a Volume II!

I was desperate to include Hanley in the book – when you mention Wigan to people the first player they automatically think of is Hanley – but unfortunately my list of contacts could not track 'The Black Pearl' down. But when you read the book I think you will find I have compiled a very good list of players who have done their best for Wigan over the years. Not that it was easy, but it has been worth it in the end.

I did have one problem with a player. One of my heroes for a short time while he was at Wigan was Bobbie Goulding. As a youngster I thought he had it all, skill, pace, arrogance and intelligence, so when a former colleague of mine, Phil Wilkinson, passed his number onto me I was made up. I phoned the number, but there was no reply – so I decided to send him a text message. I got a reply saying he would love to be involved. When I eventually got around to phoning him no-one answered, but I still kept in touch via text, but after a while I was running out of time and came to the conclusion that I was being taken for a ride and the person I was texting was not Bobbie Goulding. I still hope I am wrong, but as I never actually spoke to him I can never be 100% certain. So that was one of my setbacks which hurt for a while because

I wondered "what if I can't get anymore players and I am left with just three?"

When I wrote my first book on rugby league I called in a favour from Terry O'Connor. He provided some valuable information and I was extremely grateful. I approached the former prop-forward again to see if he was interested in helping me out once more. Terry is a man of his word and, despite his constant digs about hating me, he has never let me down yet. He was delighted to talk about his greatest Wigan game; in fact Terry is just happy when he talks. Terry also helped me get in touch with Barrie McDermott, who despite only spending one season at the club, was happy reminicising about the past.

It is hard enough trying to get in touch with players who have been away from the limelight for a number of years, but you also have to think about the games they would most likely choose. It is ok getting a star-studded list of fans' favourites, but if they do not have anything worthwhile to talk about your book is heading nowhere fast.

I had to think which games would be the crowd pullers – the Manly win in 1987, the victory over Brisbane in 1994, any one of the eight successive Challenge Cup final wins were obvious starting points. A friend of mine, Mick Hannan, got hold of Billy McGinty's number for me, so I started to think about which match he might choose. It started to become a little game for me, whenever I had secured the services of a player I had to guess which match they would choose – more often than not I was right. I know it's sad, but this has been a very stressful project and it was sending me crackers. Back to Billy; I was hoping he would choose the 1992 Challenge Cup win over Castleford at Wembley so I could ask him about his meeting with the then Prime Minister John Major that has gone down in folklore – he did not disappoint me.

All of a sudden things started to fall into place. I interviewed Dean Bell, who was very helpful, and then another friend of mine Peter Carroll got in touch with Bill Ashurst for me. Bill was brilliant and very patient with me considering the constant e-mails I have sent to him trying to get more information out of him. It got to the stage where I was thinking of ways I could get hold of players. Graeme West's granddaughter is in the same school class as my son, so I sent a letter to her dad to send on to his dad in the hope of getting an interview – and it worked because Graeme was only too happy to talk to me.

After speaking with my publisher Simon, he suggested arranging a meeting with a current Wigan player so more recent fans could relate to the book. In theory that was a great idea, but considering most of the Wigan lads now are young pups who have not won a trophy yet this was a tough task. Until I realised Sean O'Loughlin had been at the club a few years and would probably have some good tales to tell, so the press officer at Wigan Graham Emmerson helped set up a meeting with the current Wigan captain.

One friend I spoke to, who will remain nameless for obvious reasons when you read this, said "why don't you get Trent Barrett for your book? He would be great." Now Trent Barrett is one of my rugby league heroes and I would love the opportunity to interview him, but you have to remember Wigan had only signed him at the start of the 2007 season – by this time they had played just three matches – the first one we lost at home Warrington, the second one a victory in the South of France against Catalans Dragons and the third was defeat against Bradford at Odsal – not really many games he could choose to describe his 'match of my life' in a Wigan shirt! So I thanked my friend for the suggestion, but declined.

I needed to come up with a big star player who no-one would think would be possible to get hold of and would be ideal for this project – as I have said I could not get in touch with the likes of Ellery Hanley, Martin Offiah, Jason Robinson, Joe Lydon, Andrew Farrell, Kris Radlinski or Nicky Kiss, so I needed someone with the so called X-factor. Then it struck me – if I could get Brett Kenny, one of the greatest stand-offs ever to play the game, to write in my book I would feel on top of the world. Ok, back to reality. How would I get in touch in Kenny? Then I remembered he had spent the past few seasons on the coaching staff at Penrith. I emailed the media manager at the Panthers with a letter for him to pass on to Kenny – it was a long shot, but I still had hope. A day later I checked my inbox and Penrith had replied. I was delighted, but when I read the first line it said: "Brett Kenny no longer works for the club." My heart sank. I was gutted, but then I read the next line: "here is his personal email address, you can contact him on this." All of a sudden I was made up again, so I contacted him and he gladly gave me an account of his time at Wigan – and yes I did guess what game he chose.

My fiancée Christine works with Kevin Brown's brother, who used to play for Wigan, so she took him one of my letters to pass on to Kevin. I never heard anything back, so I wrote him out of my wish list. During his time at Wigan we had got to know Kevin and he was always willing to talk, so I was a little upset he had not been in touch; until, a chance meeting at Brighouse services on the M62. Wigan had just beaten Leeds in the last minute at Headingley and we decided to stop for some food on the way home. There at the services were Danny Tickle and Kevin Brown. While I was in the shop Christine collared Kevin and asked him about my letter. He said he had received it, but did not know much about it. When we explained the project he was impressed and said he would love to be involved. A few days later I interviewed Kevin and was very shocked when I asked whether he used to watch Wigan regularly, with him being from St Helens. He replied by saying "do you not remember me, I used to stand with you on the popular side at Central Park. I have always recognised your faces." Well, I was stunned to say the least. I couldn't believe I had been cheering on a player for a few years who was probably only knee high to me at Central Park and possibly guilty of spilling a number of my pints and I never recognised him.

I also contacted David Furner, who is currently assistant coach at Canberra Raiders in Australia. He replied straight away via email, but the weeks and months went by and he still had not sent me any copy for the book about his favourite match, so I thought he was out of the running because I did not want to keep pestering him; after all he was doing me a favour. But true to his word, even if it was after my initial deadline, Furner came up with the goods. I think all the grey in my hair that was starting to appear has gone now this project has ended.

I think at this time in their history Wigan rugby league need a book like this for every fan to cherish and look back on those wonderful memories.

Remember: KEEP THE FAITH.

David Kuzio
May 2007

Foreword

KEITH MILLS   Player 1967-1969

AFTER GIVING my life, well 42 years of it, to our great club, I am most honoured and privileged to be asked to provide a Foreword to David Kuzio's latest book.

'Match of my Life – Wigan Warriors' will enable me to recall and relive some magical moments with some magical people. Some of the players involved in this book stir up some wonderful recollections, not just of the games they have chosen to talk about here, but also of many other moments of glory, magic and yes, history.

Some of these players came to the club as boys, they were then shaped into men and became legends of the club and the game of rugby league. One came as a man, acted like a boy, and went away as one of the most popular players in the club's history. No prizes for guessing it was Terry O'Connor.

I was fortunate that my playing career was highlighted by appearing in teams which included the world famous legend W.J. 'Billy' Boston and 'King' Bill Ashurst. I also had the pleasure of working with stars like Brett Kenny and Dean 'The Rock' Bell later on in my career. What price would we give for another like him? Then came David Furner and Wigan's adopted son Graeme West. These are just a few of the great Antipodeans to join our club.

Local talent to make good like Shaun Edwards, Bill Ashurst, Shaun Wane and Andy Gregory were absolute masters at their trade. Emerging talent like Sean O'Loughlin (our current captain) and Kevin Brown were and are a joy to work with. How ironic that tough guy Barrie McDermott and soft lad Tez O'Connor have become a television pundit duo, every time you turn on Sky TV they are there.

All eras have a character in there ranks; cue Billy McGinty. He was a great person to have around to lighten up serious situations without taking away the intensity needed.

If this book is as successful as the players featured, it will be the result of hard work and endeavour shown by our author. There can't be a Wigan fan who won't have misty eyes and a smile on their lips after reading it.

P.S. I don't have a downer on Terry O'Connor, he will be a lasting memory for me.

Yours in Sport

Keith Mills
Former Wigan Rugby League player, Current matchday assistant and Lottery assistant in the club's Lotto shop.

THE PLAYERS

BILLY BOSTON

WINGER 1953–1968

SIGNED   From Royal Signals rugby union club

DEBUT   21 November 1953 against Barrow

WIGAN CAREER   488 appearances, 478 tries, 7 goals

HONOURS   Rugby League Championship 1959/60, Challenge Cup 1958, 1959, 1965, Lancashire Cup 1966, Lancashire League Championship 1958/59, 1961/62, Great Britain tourist 1954, 1962, Great Britain World Cup squad 1957, 1960

LEFT   Last game for Wigan was 27 April 1968 against Wakefield Trinity after he announced his retirement, but later made a surprise comeback in 1969 when he joined Blackpool Borough.

BILLY BOSTON will go down as one of the greatest wingers ever to play the game of rugby league and he is still seen as a true Wigan legend in the town today; think of Wigan rugby league club, think of the Welsh wingman Billy Boston.

Billy arrived in Wigan in 1953 and in 2007 he still lives in the town. He has a wonderful family and openly admits he could never leave Wigan as he loves it so much.

When Boston joined the Central Park club, he was being talked up as 'the next Jim Sullivan', after the legendary full-back who scored 6,022 points in his career between 1921 and 1946. This was partly also because both men began life playing rugby union in south Wales. When Boston finally made his debut for the A team against Barrow a crowd of over 8,500 people turned up to see what all the fuss was about. Over eight thousand for a reserve match was unbelievable – some Super League clubs (and champions as well) don't get that for regular home matches nowadays, never mind for a second-string side.

Boston hooked up a great partnership with another Wigan legend Eric Ashton, who was partly responsible for the winger crossing for a remarkable 478 tries in 488 appearances during his cherry and whites career. The Welshman also represented his country in 31 Test matches scoring 24 times.

After Boston retired from the game he became a pub landlord – running the Griffin at the bottom of Wigan Lane – just a stone's throw away from Central Park. This became a regular haunt for both Wigan and opposition supporters to get together before and after the game in the hope of meeting the great man. He was awarded the MBE by the Queen in June 1996 for his services to the game and is an original member of the Rugby League's Hall of Fame.

WHEN YOU have scored just short of 500 tries and won nearly every trophy in the game it would be difficult to choose one stand-out moment of such a spectacular career, but during this chapter Billy Boston will explain to you what he remembers as his most memorable game in the famous cherry and white shirt.

Boston has chosen the 1960 Championship final victory over Wakefield as his most treasured match and he explains how the coach journey over to Odsal played a major part in their triumph. He also reveals that he had never played in the wing position in his life before coming to Wigan – a position which he eventually made his own.

Despite scoring a breathtaking 478 tries for Wigan, Boston modestly says he cannot take all the credit. He believes he was just in the right place at the right time and that Eric Ashton made it a lot easier for him. I must say after looking at countless videos of Boston in action, yes Ashton was fantastic in providing the passes, but someone had to finish them off and Boston was the best in the business.

Boston played the game in the winter, so he gives his views on the summer era and whether or not he would have liked to have been part of that – I was honestly shocked by his answer.

Wigan 27 v Wakefield Trinity 3

Northern Rugby League Championship final
Saturday 21 May 1960

Odsal Stadium, Bradford
Attendance 83,190

Teams

Fred Griffiths	1	Gerry Round
Frank Halliwell	2	Fred Smith
Billy Boston	3	Alan Skene
Keith Holden	4	Neil Fox
Syd Fenton	5	John Etty
Eric Ashton	6	Ken Rollin
David Bolton	7	Keith Holiday
John Barton	8	Jack Wilkinson
Bill Sayer	9	Geoff Oakes
Frank Collier	10	Don Vines
Brian McTigue	11	Albert Firth
Geoff Lyon	12	Len Chamberlain
Roy Evans	13	Derek Turner
Boston 2, Ashton 2 Sayer	**Tries**	Smith
Griffiths 6	**Goals**	

Referee: E Clay

AMONG THE games and years I played at Wigan it is very difficult to choose just one stand-out match because I had the luxury of playing in quite a few. I spent a lot of time thinking about which game I can honestly go on record as saying was my favourite in a Wigan shirt and quite a few special occasions spring to my mind.

One was when we played Workington Town at Central Park – I think we were beating them by 40-something points – and Workington kicked the ball deep into our half and it came along to me. As I went to pick the ball up, one of the fans in the crowd shouted out, "Make it 50 Billy," and, well, I proceeded to go the length of the field to score and make it 50 just like the spectator had asked me to. Remembering things like that always make me smile because it just stands out in your memory – and that is basically what the game is about – enjoying yourself.

But the game which sticks out in my mind was when we played in the Championship final against Wakefield Trinity at Bradford in 1960. When we left Central Park I was down as number two to play on the wing, but by the time we got to Bradford I had become number three, Eric Ashton had gone from centre to number six at stand off, Dave Bolton who should have started at number six became scrum half with the number 7 shirt and they brought Frank Halliwell in to start at number two, the position I was originally down to start at.

Those were the days when the team was picked and announced a few days before the actual game, so we had one team selected when we got on the coach, but by the time we got to Yorkshire and out on the field at Odsal we had quite a few changes to the starting line up, which must have caused a few problems for Wakefield because it shocked us too.

One of the things that sticks out about that game was when I was in the dressing room before the game, our coach at the time, Joe Egan, said, "no matter if Wakefield score in the first five minutes do not worry because the longer the game goes on the more points you will score." You know being honest with you I couldn't actually work out what he meant for ages, but I managed to work it out in the end. Wakefield had played at Wembley the week before and they had been out to celebrate afterwards, so the longer the game went on the more tired they were going to get! Makes sense now doesn't it.

I scored twice in the final at Odsal. My first try came just before half time. We conceded an early try through winger Fred Smith, but Fred Griffiths kicked two penalties to give us a 4-3 lead. Then I remember receiving the ball and jinking my way past Wakefield's full-back Gerry Round to score in the corner. Griffiths added the goal and we went into the lead 9-3. My second try was an interception – their second row forward Len Chamberlain threw a ball out and I spotted this pass and caught it before the Wakefield players could get to it. I ran about 50 yards unopposed to score.

Looking back at the game on a whole it was a great game and a fantastic feeling to win the Championship. As I said, Wakefield had defeated Hull at Wembley in the Challenge Cup final the week before and I suppose they could have been feeling a little bit confident, whereas we were missing Mick Sullivan though suspension following an altercation in the semi-final. Wakefield got off to a dream start, but we did not panic, we all took on board the comments that Joe Egan had said in the dressing room about peaking at the right time.

My first try and the goals from Fred Griffiths gave us a whole lot of confidence and it was a great feeling heading into the dressing rooms at half time in the lead. In the second half I think we just blitzed them to be honest. They were struggling as their key player Neil Fox spent most of the game limping around after picking up a knock. Eric Ashton extended our lead with a brilliant piece of magic; he chipped the ball over their full-back Gerry Round's head to score. That was what Eric was like. He could produce something special out of the hat before you could blink.

Bill Sayer later escaped the clutches of Derek Turner to score from acting half-back before my interception try more or less sealed the Championship and Eric made the game safe after a neat exchange with David Bolton before sprinting 35 yards to score. I thought I played quite well that day and possibly could have had a couple of more tries if it hadn't have been for Gerry Round, who played well behind a beaten side. Credit also must go to our forwards who worked tirelessly throughout the game – John Barton, Bill Sayer, Frank Collier, Brian McTigue, Geoff Lyon and Roy Evans got through some hard work to break down the Wakefield pack which allowed myself and Eric to take advantage and score the tries.

WHEN I first came to Wigan I had never played on the wing before. Wigan put me out there to first of all learn the game, then it really became my main position. Wing might have been where I made my name, but I played in five different finals with Wigan playing in five different positions, although I played in a lot more than five finals altogether. Before I joined Wigan I was regularly playing rugby for the army at centre, before that though I was a full-back. I even played full-back for the Wales Boys Club, but that was rugby union.

I got asked quite a lot at the time about what my reaction was to being stuck out on the wing in a position and a game that I had never played. It didn't really bother me, though. A lot of it is luck if you know what I mean; although you do tend to make your own luck.

When I signed, the Wigan team of that time was splitting up. There was a mixture of players retiring or signing for other clubs. I was 19 when I signed. I go back to my earlier luck comment here; with my first touch on my debut for the club I scored my first try. I didn't actually beat anyone for that try, just accepted the pass at the right time. This happened again when I played my first game at international level. I received the ball for the first time and scored my first international try. I did not really do anything, just like the Wigan game I just finished off the move. Things like that, though, give you the confidence to aim high and achieve more in your short time playing the game.

LIKE I said earlier, I came over to Wigan as a 19 year-old rugby union player to a place that was foreign to me really and I was treated very well by the club, the fans and the people of Wigan. Everything just seemed right. It was great. The other players were brilliant to me and they helped me slot in better. It really does help you settle in when you get a good bunch of lads plus, I was on the wing and you are out of the way sort of thing when the really hard stuff starts flying.

My first ever game in a Wigan shirt was an academy team game away at Barrow. There were around 8,500 fans watching the game that day – at the time I did not know what sort of gate the A teams were getting. 8,500 fans was a massive crowd for that type of game. It's a big crowd for a first team game these days. The massive crowd really didn't bother me – I was more nervous about just playing the game. I was not concerned or really focusing on the crowd being honest with you. I just wanted to get used to the game and was more concerned with that. As a player your main intention is to play well and help your team win, the crowd and things like that take care of themselves.

It has been mentioned that people had already started to compare me with the likes of the legendary Jim Sullivan, but it didn't affect me. Luckily enough I was in the army and I only arrived in Wigan a few hours before the game, so I never heard what people were saying about me – whether I was going to be as good or as bad as players who had played for Wigan before me. I just came in for the first game and went to the dressing room to find our jerseys were all laid out for us. As a player then we didn't really have to do much before the game; your boots were cleaned for you and your socks were on your peg just waiting for you. Everything was there that you needed. All you had to do was sit down and prepare yourself for the game ahead.

I will always have great memories of my time as a Wigan player and Wigan itself. I still live in the town today. My life has evolved here, I got married here, all my children were born here and I've even run a pub in the town. I've had some wonderful times in Wigan.

I had a fantastic career in rugby league. I won a lot of trophies during my time in Wigan, I represented Great Britain 31 times, won the World Cup, and I played for the nationalities and played in numerous cup finals. I don't think there was a cup final that I played with Wigan that we didn't win. We won the Lancashire Cup final, the Championship final, Championship play-off final and the Challenge Cup. I also was a part of the Great Britain side that won the Ashes – so it wasn't a bad career really.

LOOKING AT rugby league nowadays compared to when I played the game, I suppose I do wish we would have been given the chance to play in something like the World Club Challenge, but having said that we did play the Australians at Central Park and we beat them. We played New Zealand and beat them as well, so it was not like we didn't play the best teams around. It was just not the format of the current World Club Challenge where the champions of the Super League play the champions of the NRL either over here or in Australia. I suppose at the time we could have called ourselves the champions of the world after beating both them sides, but it wasn't something we thought about at the time.

Obviously I played the game in winter era compared with today's summer era. I am being totally honest with you here, I don't think I would have liked to play in the modern game. I would sooner play in the good old days. Listen I was a wingman and we always saw the ball, that's why we scored so many times. The wingers hardly see the ball these days; they have to go inside now to get the ball or spend half their time chasing it about until they receive a pass. In my day we had Eric Ashton making the break and I was there to finish it off. If Eric made a break or even half a break I would always be alongside him, but in Super League it's all up the middle. It's mainly the scrum-halves who are topping the try scoring lists now. Denis Moran topped the list for two years on the trot when he played for the London Broncos, then you've got Danny McGuire at Leeds Rhinos, he's topped it as well, but he did it from stand-off. Even Kris Radlinski, when he was full-back at Wigan, topped the list with most tries one season. It has been a while since a winger has come top, I think Lesley Vanikolo has done it once, but when I played I never remember any other position than winger topping the try-scoring lists and I played for over 20 years. It was always a winger that won that particular honour in those days.

At the moment there is a lad at Wigan called Mark Calderwood. He must be one of the fastest wingers in the game, but he does not get put into positions where he can use his speed and score over 20 or 30 tries a season. In my day we had players who would look for the winger all the time – that's what is missing from Super League.

I still go watching Wigan even now and I know things have not gone well in recent years, but I don't necessarily think we have been in a slump, I honestly think they do not have the incentive to play anymore. The players today get paid whether they play or not and when they are playing they get the same wage win, lose of draw. For those who don't know, in my day there was winning pay and losing pay. There was always a difference between winning and losing when it came to the money you received at the end of the week. That is not in the game anymore, I'm not saying that is the sole cause of the recent problems at Wigan, but I'm sure that it does not help.

I enjoy watching the game and I will always love my rugby league, I'd rather watch rugby league any day than rugby union that's for sure. Even though I have played both codes it is very rare that I watch rugby union. It's not something I would rush home to watch on the television, you know what I'm saying. When I played rugby union and we were on the back-line, you could go behind the sticks and have a cigarette because you never saw the ball; the forwards never parted with it. I never had that problem, though, when I played for Wigan. I always saw the ball as my try scoring record proves and I would not have it any other way. There is nothing worse than spending 80 minutes out in the mud and rain and not receiving a pass all game – where is the enjoyment in that?

For all that, though, I love remembering the good old days and that victory in the final against Wakefield just about makes it as my greatest game. It was a close run thing, though, as we had so many great games throughout my time at the club. It was great to be part of it.

BILL ASHURST

SECOND ROW/THREE-QUARTER 1968–73/1977-78

SIGNED   From amateur club Rose Bridge

DEBUT   7 September 1968 against St Helens

WIGAN CAREER   186 appearances, 74 tries, 152 goals

HONOURS   League Leaders Trophy 1970/71, Lancashire Cup 1971,
Lancashire League Championship 1969/70, BBC2 Floodlit Trophy 1968

LEFT   Joined Penrith in 1973 before rejoining Wigan in 1977, his final
game ever for the Wigan was 11 March 1978 against Bradford Northern

IT IS very difficult writing about a player you never really got to see in his pomp, and Bill Ashurst is one of those players who falls into that category. Many people I have spoken to who remember Ashurst during his two spells at the club rate him as one of the best ball-handling and tactical kicking second-row forwards this country has ever seen. Ashurst joined the club as a centre, but he was eventually moved into the pack where he formed a formidable partnership with Dave Robinson and Doug Laughton.

After terrorising defences up and down the country Ashurst put himself in the shop window with a marvellous performance against a touring Australia side and eventually in 1973 Ashurst joined Australian club side Penrith Panthers for a then world record fee of £15,000. He took the Australian game by storm, but caused an upset when he walked out on the club to return to England in 1977.

Shortly after arriving back home Ashurst rejoined Wigan and his final game for the club came against Bradford Northern, when a half-time bust-up with coach Vince Karalius saw Ashurst refuse to play the second half. He then left the club a couple of days later to join Wakefield Trinity for another record fee of £18,000.

Ashurst made three appearances for Great Britain and after he retired he eventually became coach of Runcorn Highfield. At the time Runcorn were probably rated as the worst team in rugby league. Ashurst transformed the club, but that only resulted in an astonishing reason for being dismissed by the club.

BILL ASHURST always believed he was good enough to mix it with the best rugby league players in the world and in 1972 he finally got the chance to prove it. Wigan took on Australia in a match at Central Park and this was a chance for Ashurst to showcase his talent against players like Bobby Fulton, Mark Harris, Tommy Raudonikis and Arthur Beetson – he never disappointed.

Ashurst had an outstanding game and is still aggrieved now all these years later that Wigan did not win the game. Ashurst became the first player ever to win the Harry Sunderland Man of the Match award for being on the losing side in the Championship final.

In this chapter Ashurst recalls his memories of the game and how that performance opened many avenues in his career which saw him rated as the best forward in both England and Australia.

Wigan 18 v Australia 18

1972 Tour match
Saturday 17 November 1972

Central Park, Wigan
Attendance not recorded

Teams

Colin Tyrer	1	Ray Branighan
Kevin O'Loughlin	2	John Grant
Dave Hill	3	Bobby Fulton
Bill Francis	4	Geoff Starling
Kieron O'Loughlin	5	Mark Harris
Bill Davies	6	Tommy Raudonikis
Jimmy Nulty	7	Dennis Ward
Alan Bence	8	John O'Neil
Colin Clarke	9	Fred Jones
Laurie Hinchcliffe	10	Bob O'Reilly
Bill Ashurst	11	Arthur Beetson
Dave Robinson	12	Gary Stevens
Doug Laughton	13	Gary Sullivan
	Substitutes	
Eddie Cunningham	14	Paul Sait
Terry Cramant	15	Elwyn Walters
Hill, O'Loughlin	**Tries**	Fulton 3, Starling
Tyrer 4	**Goals**	Branighan 3
Ashurst 2	**Drop Goals**	

THE GAME I can say was one of my favourites in a Wigan shirt would have to be when we played against the touring Australia side in 1972 at Central Park.

The build-up to the match was special for me because I had never played against a top class side like that before, even though I had played against top class domestic opposition all year. I'd missed out on the previous Great Britain tour because the coaching committee did not think I'd had enough experience to handle those types of games – instead they took the other two back-row forwards who were playing with me at Wigan at the time in Doug Laughton and David Robinson.

That particular year I had won 40-odd Man of the Match awards and was playing some really good rugby, so to get a chance to play against a side like Australia was just awesome. I mean they had some outstanding players in their party, such as Graham Langlands, Bobby Fulton, Mark Harris, Tommy Raudonikis, Ronnie Coote and Arthur Beetson.

The game was at Central Park on Friday November 17th 1972 and in the end we drew 18-18. It was just an awesome experience and I honestly felt I had a terrific game that night; I felt I belonged on the big stage playing against players like that.

I also got the Man of the Match award for that game as well and looking back we should have beaten the Aussies. I remember our loose-forward Doug Laughton throwing out an interception pass to Bobby Fulton, who would later become the Australia coach after he retired from playing, to run away and score. Then Fulton grabbed his second try from another interception pass – this time I think it was Bill Davies, so they actually scored 10 points they didn't really earn. In those days it was three points for a try instead of the four you receive today and two for the conversion, so we really gifted them so many points the result could and should have been different that night.

From my personal point of view my kicking game was absolutely awesome – in our day we did not have the 40-20 rule like they use nowadays to benefit the kicking team – but I kicked really well and I must have hit quite few "40-20s" that night. My general play was also out of this world. There was one incident during the game when I got the ball in my own 22 did a neat little chip over the top. I raced through to collect the ball and I approached their full-back Ray Branighan before drawing him in and then I put Kevin O'Loughlin over for his try. I actually created all our tries that night. It was such a fantastic feeling to be able to pit your wits against world class players at that time.

That game at Central Park was a major stepping stone in my career because from that match I was recommended to play for Australian clubs. At that time a lot of clubs were signing English players because the players down under could not play the way we did – they played their typical style of Australian football, which was plenty of power, strength and pace, but no brains. I received some good offers, but I eventually agreed to sign for the Penrith in 1973.

I ended up spending four years in Australia playing week in week out against top class players basically all on the back of one game over in England at Central Park.

GOING INTO that game against Australia I felt I had a point to prove to the English rugby league after being overlooked by my country. Actually after that game I was selected to play for Great Britain during the World Cup tournament in France, but unfortunately I had done my cruciate knee ligament and I could not play. I was also in dispute with Wigan at the time, so I didn't play for Great Britain in the World Cup final. The team drew with Australia which saw us win the trophy after having a better record against our opponents in the group stages – I only played for Great Britain on three occasions, so I suppose I am a bit miffed I never really got to showcase my talents on the international scene, although I did manage to do it on the other side of the world.

My first spell at Wigan was from 1968 until 1973. Then I signed for Penrith in Australia in a bid to really test myself. I had always wanted to play against the best in the world and to keep challenging myself. That was always my aim throughout my career. At that particular time I was rated as one of the best back-row forwards in the world and when I went over to Australia I had that tag for another three or four years.

My second spell at Central Park came after I left Penrith. I was experiencing a few problems back home and I decided to come back. I asked Penrith for some leave so I could see my family and sort my life out, but they refused. Well I was not standing for that, so I just packed my bags and got on a plane and flew back to England without a word. It is funny because I have just been back to Penrith after 30 years – they had just picked their best ever legends team and I was selected in the second-row which is a fabulous achievement really. I am so proud of that because Penrith have had some wonderful forwards over the years and it is very rare that a Pom is chosen over an Aussie in anything, so yeah it is great to be a Hall of Famer in the history of such a great club like Penrith and they only picked a squad of 17 which makes it more enjoyable.

When I left Penrith I did not have a club to go back to. I just got on a plane and came home. One of the directors at Penrith told me about a story which happened very shortly after he discovered I had walked out. He went home that night and his wife was complaining she was not feeling very clever. She was suffering from some severe chest pains and she said to him, "I am not well, I think I am dying, I am having a heart attack," things like that. He just replied back, "never mind your heart attack. Bill Ashurst has just flown home." He was a lovely bloke and his wife has actually confirmed that story that he was more concerned that I had left the club and was ignoring the fact his wife could have been having a heart attack!

I THEN re-signed for Wigan. At the time Vince Karalius was coach and he was probably one of the best fitness coaches I had ever trained under, but as far as football was concerned we did not see eye-to-eye. I was always an off-the-cuff kind of player. It was just all spontaneous with me and he did not want me playing that type of rugby while he was in charge. I remember we were playing against Bradford in a cup game at Central Park and I came off at half time. During the first half I'd worked a set piece and threw an inside ball back to Steve O'Neill who went in under the posts. Vince Karalius grabbed hold of me at half time and said, "I do not want you throwing passes like that." I said, "well, you will get no more from me then, I want out of this club."

That was on the Saturday; on the Sunday I turned down an offer from Hull, but on the Monday I got a visit from Wakefield Trinity chairman Trevor Woodward and David Topliss, who I had played with at Penrith. We agreed terms and on that same day I left Wigan again for a record fee – I think it was £18,000. When I'd left Wigan to join Penrith that was also a record fee at the time worth $27,000 (£15,000) so I commanded two world transfer fees during my career. That proved I was not a bad player.

There was another occasion during my Wigan career that stands out. It was when I was chosen as the Harry Sunderland Trophy winner for man-of-the-match in the 1971 Championship Final against St Helens, which was a great honour – the only problem was that we lost the game.

It was not the losing that was incredibly hard to take, but the manner in which we lost it. I was having a terrific game that day and I was also the second choice goal kicker. Our full-back Colin Tyrer, who by the way was a tremendous player, had a really off day with his kicking, I believe he missed seven shots at goal and I begged my captain Dougie Laughton to let me kick, but my plea fell on deaf ears.

I think I dropped two goal kicks that day and also scored a try. My try was a great feeling because we were well on top and it came just after to half time, I also had a hand in our opening try where I glided through the St Helens defence before putting Dave Robinson over the line. I took great pride in setting up tries for Wigan. It is good to score yourself, but when you know you helped create special tries that can be just as rewarding.

We worked so hard to get into a winning position that day, but during the last two minutes St Helens' Jonnie Walsh attempted a drop at goal, which missed, and our winger Stuart Wright allowed the ball to bounce. It landed in the hands of the Saints centre Billy Benyon, who we knew to be 10 yards offside. It was devastating when Mr Lawrensen, the referee, awarded the try I could not believe it.

I think I kicked the post so hard out of sheer disappointment that I damaged my ankle. There was no time left to kick off as the final whistle went after the conversion, so you can see how close we came to winning. I think the ref was retired after that game due to bad eyesight.

To win the Man of the Match, I suppose to many other players it would have been a fantastic achievement, but to me it was scant reward after losing the game. Do not get me wrong I am really proud to have won the Harry Sunderland Trophy. It wasn't just for me, but also for my team mates as well because I could not have won it without there help. But it is not something you like to sing from the rooftops when you have just been beaten in the last minute of a major final against your arch-rivals St Helens.

I ENDED up making a final appearance at Central Park when I was the coach of Runcorn Highfield. It was a twist of fate that ended up with me actually being on the field. The year before Runcorn had had a great year, I think they had won about four games in four years before I took over, but I changed that and we had been winning quite a few matches. But in the week building up to the game some of the players went on strike because the club would not up their match money, even though we were playing Wigan, so I went on the substitutes' bench. The rest is history really because the majority of people in rugby league will know that I did not last very long when I got on to the field of play that day as I was sent off following an altercation with Wigan's second-row forward Andy Goodway.

At the end of that season with Runcorn it was funny because the chairman called me into his office and said, "we are going to have to release you Billy!" I said, "why? What's wrong our results are good." And quick as a flash he replied, "That's the problem, Billy. We cannot afford to keep paying winning money." So I left the game after that. I suppose I was a victim of my own success.

Being a Wigan lad it was an absolutely awesome feeling being able to represent the club. The second highlight of my career was not actually in a competitive league or cup game – it was a testimonial match. One of my all-time heroes ever at Wigan is probably everyone else's and that is Billy Boston. He asked me to play centre to him in his benefit game and I jumped at the chance. It was a major highlight to play with someone I had idolised since I was 10 years-old in the hen-pen at Central Park, so to get the opportunity to rub shoulders with him and pass him the ball was a real honour. I actually told him, "don't retire Billy and I'll make you a star," but he wouldn't listen to me.

Also having the opportunity to play with Eric Ashton in that same benefit match was just fantastic. I used to idolise all those players in the sixties, in fact I went on to meet them all in the bar and had some crazy drinking nights with them.

The two most awesome players that I played against were former Great Britain coach Malcolm Reilly, who played out in Australia for Manly when I was in Penrith and an Australian called Arthur Beetson. I met them both again recently when I went back to Australia. It was great to catch up and talk about the good old times and to compare the scars that we gave each other, for as you know it was a brutal game then when we played and there was no quarter asked and none given.

There was one game when I was playing for Penrith that my mum went onto the field and walloped the referee! We were playing North Sydney Bears at Penrith Park when an almighty brawl ensued; I think 26 players were scrapping. When it all calmed down my mum went onto the field and hit the referee with her handbag. His name was Donald McDonald, so you can see he was only one letter short of being a clown in the first place. Any way my mum timed it just right as the day in question that this incident occurred on was Mother's Day.

The next game we played was against Eastern Suburbs, who had a wonderful team, with the likes of Bobby Fulton, Ron Coote, Fairfax, Harris and Mullins to name a few and, of course, a certain Mr Arthur Beetson. At the first scrum it erupted and me and Artie squared up to each other, but before either could throw a punch Ronnie Coote bobbed up from loose-forward and shouted, "don't hit him Art or he will send for his mum!" So I then spent the entire game chasing Cootie, so I could smack him one.

I met him on my recent trip to Australia and the first thing he said was, "how is your mum?" God Bless Him – which I did not actually say at the time.

GRAEME WEST

SECOND ROW/PROP FORWARD 1982–91

SIGNED   From Hawera in New Zealand

DEBUT   21 November 1982 against Leeds

WIGAN CAREER   202 appearances, 49 tries

HONOURS   World Club Challenge 1987, Rugby League Championship 1986/87, Challenge Cup 1985, Premiership Trophy 1987, John Player Special Trophy 1982/83, 1984/85, 1985/86, Lancashire Cup 1986, 1986, Charity Shield 1985, 1987. New Zealand tourist 1975, 1980, 1982

LEFT   Became player-coach for the A team in 1988, but his final appearance for the first-team was 21 April 1991 versus Featherstone Rovers at Central Park.

GRAEME WEST will go down in history as one of the greatest foreign imports ever to represent Wigan. He wasn't one of your high-flying superstars who would race 80 yards to score – he was a typical hard-working forward who never took a backward step and was never frightened to put his body on the line.

After his immense playing career ended, West took over the role of player-coach of the A team at Central Park and continued to turn out for them in a bid to help his youngsters through the matches. He also coached a number of talented youngsters who eventually got promoted to the first-team before either becoming regulars at Wigan or kickstarting their careers somewhere else.

After being a huge success as the A team boss West was handed the reigns as first-team coach when the club parted company with John Dorahy. He then guided Wigan to the Premiership Trophy and also become coach of the first English team to win the World Club Championship on Australian soil by beating Brisbane Broncos.

WIGAN HAD reached the Challenge Cup final in 1984, but were well beaten by an impressive Widnes side. So less than 12 months later the Central Park outfit had the opportunity to set the record straight by returning to Wembley and lifting the Challenge Cup for their loyal fans. But in their way stood a tough and talented Hull Kingston Rovers team.

The semi-final was a hard-fought encounter which tested Wigan's defence that was superbly marshalled by one Graeme West, but they managed to hold on in a memorable finale to set up a final clash with Hull FC.

In this chapter West remembers the feeling about reaching Wembley again and also about his coaching career as the club's A team boss and the first-team after John Dorahy was sacked.

He also reveals his pride at seeing son Dwayne do well in Super League before having to retire from injury.

Wigan 18 v Hull Kingston Rovers 11

Challenge Cup semi-final
Saturday 23 March 1985

Elland Road, Leeds
Attendance 19,275

Teams

Shaun Edwards	1	George Fairbairn
Brian Juliff	2	Garry Clark
David Stephenson	3	Ian Robinson
Steve Donlan	4	Gary Prohm
Henderson Gill	5	John Lydiat
Brett Kenny	6	Mike Smith
Mike Ford	7	Paul Harkin
Neil Courtney	8	Mark Broadhurst
Nicky Kiss	9	David Watkinson
Brian Case	10	Zook Ema
Graeme West	11	Phil Hogan
Shaun Wane	12	Andy Kelly
Ian Potter	13	Gavin Miller
	Substitutes	
Mick Scott	14	Gordon Smith
Colin Whitfield	15	Dave Hall
Gill, Stephenson Juliff	**Tries**	Miller, Clark
Stephenson 2, Gill	**Goals**	Fairbairn
	Drop Goals	Harkin

Referee: R Campbell

I HAVE to say that the 1985 Challenge Cup final victory over Hull at Wembley was one of my stand-out moments in my career. It was a really good team performance that day. But actually the semi-final that secured our passage to the final was really special. We beat Hull Kingston Rovers at Elland Road in Leeds. That was a real good match; they were favourites to reach the final and we were up against it a wee bit really. The game itself was a real see-saw battle. They were in front, then we went in front, they then regained the lead before we hit back again. It was a fantastic game and all the spectators were going bananas in the stands and at the end when we had won, which took us back to Wembley, that was a hell of a feeling, you know.

Trying to think back about that game I kind of remember one of our wingers, Brian Juliff, scoring one of the tries on the right hand side. Our centre David Stephenson scored following a break from me down the right hand side – as I made the break he came up and supported me before collecting the ball and crossing over the line. Henderson Gill was also on the scoresheet that day when he scored down the left hand side in a move which also involved me.

I think there was an incident late in the game where Brett Kenny threw out a wild pass that was intercepted by the Rovers attack, but fortunately we thwarted them. That was one of the games where he really didn't fire you know. He defended well, but a lot did not come off for him in attack. In most of the games in which Kenny played he was a fantastic pivot; he scored tries himself and also set up plenty by sending great balls out to the outside backs to score. To be fair, when we turned up for the final Brett played exceptionally well and won the Lance Todd Trophy award for the man-of-the-match, but in the semi-final at Leeds, for whatever reason, he just did not fire as well as he usually did. But the team came through in the end with a superb effort.

THE YEAR before we had been in the Challenge Cup final against local rivals Widnes and they'd really turned us over, so I suppose that was on our minds. It was unbelievable really because I had been sent a letter after the 1984 final; a Reverend had written to me, I forget where he was from but it was down south somewhere. He said how disappointed about the final he and his friends were, and all that, after going to the game. I decided to write back to him and I sent him the same letter back with a note on the bottom: "do not worry. We will get back again next year."

And to be honest I didn't give it much thought after that. But when we got back to Wembley and then went on to beat Hull to win the Challenge Cup the following year, he wrote back to me saying how much he'd enjoyed it, adding his note to the bottom of the same letter, that I replied to, saying "paid in full. Marvelous performance". It was unbelievable that this bloody letter had gone backwards and forwards three times.

Going back to the semi-final, when the final whistle went it was fantastic to know we were going back to Wembley again. We were all up for it this time because we were playing some great stuff. We had Brett Kenny playing some of his best ever rugby, we had John Ferguson and Henderson Gill on the wings, and there was a young Shaun Edwards at full-back. At that time we had a good forward pack – there was Neil Courtney at prop with Brian Case. Ian Potter was playing and we had Nicky Kiss at hooker. Like I said, our pack was strong and could hold their own and we had a back line that could do anything and score from anywhere. That year I think both our wingers Ferguson and Gill were in the top five try-scorers for the season, so it showed we were playing entertaining rugby.

TO PLAY at a stadium like Wembley is fantastic because it is so big, but truthfully it is like any other game – if you are not playing well on the day the whole occasion drains the energy out of you. In the 1984 final we did not stand a chance; Widnes were just too good for us.

Considering the games we won to reach the final in '84 we just did not play when it really mattered. The ball seemed to stop around the halves and we never got around to where we could actually do anything to cause our opponents any real problems.

In 1985 we went out and played brilliant rugby in the first half, but in the second half Hull started to come back at us a bit. In the end we had just done enough to win the game – but it was getting very close at the death. James Leuluai, the father of Wigan's current scrum-half Thomas, scored a great try. Then they made another break down the left hand side right at the end of the game, but we managed to bring them down and the hooter went. We were really relieved. It was just one of those games were the first half was ours and the second-half was theirs.

I know a lot of past players go on about it, but the homecomings were very special to us. I remember coming back from the 1984 defeat – that was the second final I had ever played in for Wigan, the first was when we won the John Player Special Trophy – but having lost a Wembley I was on the coach on the way home thinking "Christ, we haven't played very well." And being honest we just wanted to get home, but when we arrived at Central Park the staff came out and said "geez. You'd better get out on the park. They have come down to welcome you home" – and I'm thinking "they can't have, the way we played in that game, no way could anyone be there." But I walked out and there was around four or five thousand people there and this was when we lost. I just could not believe it. That really made all the players think we had to get back to Wembley and try to make it right by winning the Challenge Cup as soon as possible. Fortunately we did just that 12 months later.

I MADE a decision when I signed a five-year contract with Wigan that wild horses would not take me home, I was going to stay and make it over here if it killed me. There was no way I was going to go back home to New Zealand having people tell me that I could not do it and I could not hack it. So for those five years I was definitely going to be here and whatever I needed to do I was going to do it to be successful in rugby league. So basically it just carried on from there and I still live in Wigan now. When I first came over I liked the place straightaway. I like the area and I love the people, so I do not have a problem living in Wigan it is a great place to be in.

It is not just my playing career that I look on with fond memories. I also coached the A team – which was the second team at Wigan – from 1988 until 1994. I was still playing, so I was player-coach in the A team for quite a few years. I was playing prop and I was out there really just helping some of the younger guys out and getting them through the games to give them a bit of guidance not just off the park but on it as well. I enjoyed it as there were a lot of young players that came through that went on to play for the first team and excelled for Wigan. Also there were a lot of players who came in and then left for other clubs and they did well when they left Wigan. you had the likes of Scott Naylor, Mike Forshaw, Longy and Gildart. Augustine O'Donnell went to St Helens, but he had a problem with his kidneys. They either made it in the first team at Central Park or they left and excelled at other clubs. It was satisfying for me as a coach and it was very good for the team as well. Some of them had to leave because Wigan had a lot of players in their positions who were still young themselves and couldn't get through, so they tried their luck elsewhere and for some of them it paid off. I did have some players who got a bit disillusioned; they were the ones you worried about because they would say "I can't do this, I can't do that".

There were a lot of different players that filed through the A team around the same time – at one stage there was the likes of Ian Lucas, Denis Betts and Phil Clarke – they all went through together and we were sort of threadbare for players for a while and then the likes of Ian Gildart, Mick Cassidy, Andy Farrell and Mike Forshaw all started to come through and the A team started to do well again until it was their turn to push their way into the first team equation. Then it continued again. We had Sean Long, Augustine O'Donnell and Wayne Reid who started coming through, so throughout my time there were different waves of players coming through. I think we won the Challenge Cup and the League for the A team at one time and the Lancashire Cup, which was done with one set of players as well. In my last year as coach, with the likes of Longy and Ducky in the side, we finished second in the league.

AFTER MY success with the A team I made the step up to first-team coach. I was quite lucky really because, having been in charge of them, I knew all the players at the club. I knew their capabilities and the weaknesses. When John Monie left the club he asked me if I wanted him to recommend me for the job – I said "no". I had a testimonial that year and I did not want to combine that with being coach of the first team. They then brought in John Dorahy, who was not really that successful and in the end they sacked him. I'm not sure how it came about but I think they reluctantly came to me and said "do you want to take the job over until the end of the season?" I said "yeah, I'll give it a shot." I was very lucky to take over a very good bunch of players. I also knew who was coming through from underneath at A team level which was a bonus.

We had some very good players at Wigan during that time. They knew how to play the game and in any team if you have intelligent players that know the set up and how the game is played on the park, not just for their own position but they know how the team plays, you are quids in really.

This was in 1994 and we had to go to Brisbane for the World Club Challenge, but the weekend before we had just won the Premiership trophy. What was a bit disjointing was that Kelvin Skerrett got injured; he broke his jaw and could not go to Brisbane. At that time Dean Bell and Andy Platt were both a big part of the team, but they also ended up not going to Australia. Before we got there Martin Dermott and Barrie-Jon Mather were both struggling with injuries, so we had to put a makeshift team together – that makeshift team turned out to be world beaters. I think our prop forward Neil Cowie led from the front that night and it was probably the best game I had ever seen him play. He almost took the Brisbane pack on all by himself. Also Billy McGinty, who had been injured all year and had not played much, was usually a second rower, but he had to fill in at blind-side prop and went as far as he could go. He did marvelously well; as did the rest of the team including Clarkey, Betts, Farrell, Shaun Edwards and Sam Panapa, it was just a fantastic performance.

LOOKING BACK at my career I played with some good players at Wigan and I also coached some special ones too, but I think in those days Shaun Edwards was one of the true greats. He came into the team as a very young player and at the beginning he was asked to fill in a few positions. He went from stand-off to centre, then from wing to full-back and back to stand-off, but they stuck with him and he turned into one of the best players and one of the best half backs I have ever seen. I think it was great that Wigan kept with him – in this day and age clubs tend to give a player a few games and then dispatch with him straight away which is a bit soul-destroying really. I think some of the players Wigan have got rid of would be better if they had been given the opportunity to play a bit more, maybe in different positions or a few games in the first team then drop them back to the reserves, but it just does not happen these days. I know I played with great players like Andy Gregory, Dean Bell, Ellery Hanley and Joe Lydon, but being honest Shaun Edwards has to be the best player I have ever had the privilege of playing with.

I would have loved to have played in the summer months, you have to remember the conditions we played in during the winter, all the crap we had to plough through. I used to think "I'm freezing to death out here, what am I doing?" When my career came to an end that is when summer rugby finally arrived, so yes I would've loved to have been able to play on dry tracks to see what it was like.

I've been proud of my son Dwayne's career as well as my own. At a young age Dwayne did not really take to the game, his defence was not really good. He was at Ashton for a while then went to St Pats. He was coached under Derek Birchall at Deanery High School and Derek was a real stalwart of the game. When he got hold of Dwayne he transformed him. I was quite surprised when I went to watch him compared to what he was like the year before – he had been turned into a good defender and had a very good step on him – the transformation was amazing.

It was good to watch him. When he got to Wigan he did not get the opportunity to go into any easy matches so to speak and be allowed to play his natural game. He got stuck straight in against St Helens in a match Wigan were struggling to win and he didn't play so well that first time, which knocked him back a bit. He then went to St Helens and was given the opportunity to display his skills. He was doing all right until he did his shoulder and had to have two major operations and was eventually forced to give the game away, but he is still involved in rugby league helping me coach at St Judes.

One of my proud moments watching Dwayne was a try he was involved in playing for St Helens, I think it has been voted one of the best tries in the Super League era. It was against Bradford and I remember the commentator Eddie Hemmings shouting "It's wide to West". He kept repeating it and eventually Dwayne got the ball out to Chris Joynt who scored the winning try. It was great for Dwayne to be involved in something like that. I think what ever happens in life happens. You have to accept it and get on with life. It is no good looking back and being envious about anybody, you have got to say "I did what I did and I enjoyed the fight and I am getting on with my life," and that is what me and Dwayne have done since our rugby league careers came to an end. He even said to me a few months ago "do you think I could go on and play again? What do think?"

I said "are you enjoying your coaching?" He said "yeah, I'm just getting a bit frustrated with the team not doing so well and I think I could help out". I basically just told him that is part of being a coach. You have to be very patient and work with your players. Improvement will not happen overnight, but if you keep working with them then it will get better and he is now starting to see the results and they are starting to get better and he's more satisfied. That is part and parcel of the game. Once you have had your lot you have had your lot.

Luckily for me, my lot included a wonderful career with some fantastic memories.

BRETT KENNY

STAND-OFF 1984–85

SIGNED   16 November 1984 From Parramatta Eels – off season deal from
          ARL club

DEBUT   9 December 1984 v Warrington

WIGAN CAREER   25 appearances, 19 tries

HONOURS   Challenge Cup 1985

LEFT   May 1985 to return to Australia for start of ARL season

BRETT KENNY arrived at Central Park in an off-season deal from Australian Rugby League giants Parramatta in a common arrangement which saw top Test players come over to England for a few months to keep them fit after the ARL had finished for the season. Kenny was one of the best stand-offs in the world in 1984/85 and after his brief stint at Wigan he returned back down under and continued to be one of the greatest for club and country.

Kenny represented Australia 17 times between 1982 and 1987 and was also part of the 1982 Invincibles and the 1986 Unconquerables Ashes Tours to Great Britain. Kenny was also a crucial member of the New South Wales team – playing in the stand-off role or even at centre and he had some memorable battles against Queensland greats such as Wally Lewis and Mal Meninga.

In this chapter Kenny recalls his brief stint in England and squashes the well-publicised rumours surrounding his exit from Central Park.

AFTER DEFEATING Hull Kingston Rovers 18-11 in the Challenge Cup semi-final at Elland Road – the home of Leeds United football club – Wigan made a swift return to the Twin Towers 12 months after crashing to a 19–6 loss at the hands of local rivals Widnes in the 1984 Challenge Cup final. Confidence was high within the camp at Wigan with coaches Alan McInnes and Colin Clarke boasting an array of stars including Brett Kenny, John Ferguson, Graeme West and the talented youngster Shaun Edwards, but standing in the way were Arthur Bunting's Airlie Birds, who were relying on the skills of Kenny's Parramatta and Australia team-mate Peter Sterling, and the talented New Zealand quartet of James Leuluai, Dane O'Hara, Fred Ah Kuoi and Gary Kemble to help them bring home the trophy they had last won in 1982.

The final was set up to be a classic – and it didn't disappoint.

Wigan 28 v Hull 24

Challenge Cup final
Saturday 4 May 1985

Wembley Stadium
Attendance 97,801

Teams

Shaun Edwards	1	Gary Kemble
John Ferguson	2	Kevin James
David Stephenson	3	Steve Evans
Steve Donlan	4	James Leuluai
Henderson Gill	5	Dane O'Hara
Brett Kenny	6	Fred Ah Kuoi
Mike Ford	7	Peter Sterling
Neil Courtney	8	Lee Crooks
Nicky Kiss	9	Shaun Patrick
Brian Case	10	Neil Puckering
Graeme West	11	John Muggleton
Brian Dunn	12	Paul Rose
Ian Potter	13	Steve Norton
	Substitutes	
Nicky Du Toit	14	Garry Schofield
Danny Campbell	15	Gary Divorty
Ferguson, Edwards Gill, Kenny	**Tries**	James 2, Evans Leuluai 2, Divorty
Gill 3, Stephenson	**Goals**	Crooks 2

Referee: R Campbell

IT WAS back in 1984 when a number of my Parramatta team-mates had signed to play with clubs in the English premiership. I had not even contemplated playing in England at club level, although I had already toured there with the Kangaroos in 1982. At Parramatta the players and their partners were very close and socialised a lot together. It was on one of these social outings that the players and their partners who were going to England started to work on myself and my fiancée, Julie, about how great it would be to have us going to England as well, particularly considering we were to be married in October of that year and it could be an extended honeymoon for us.

Julie was keen to go as she had never been to England and thought it would be great to experience life in another country. So, after some persuasion, I agreed to look for a club to play with. I was thinking I would probably be playing with some of my team-mates at one of the clubs they had signed with. A friend of mine, John White, had done some negotiating for the other guys, so he looked around for me. Wigan were the club with an opening for an overseas import, so that's why I signed and I couldn't have been happier with the warm welcome and acceptance of the Wigan club, supporters and the Wigan people.

My first game for Wigan was against Warrington. This, of course, was a local derby and the players were telling me how much both team's supporters hated each other, that fights would break out in the crowd. Well, it wasn't just off the field where the action was happening; there were a few things happening on the field as well. I recall running slightly across field to link up with our other Aussie John Ferguson. As I flicked the ball back inside to him the Warrington player trailing me connected with me with a nice elbow to the head well after I had passed the ball. I guess it was a 'Welcome to England' gesture, which I still had with me for a couple of days after the game.

MY MOST memorable game was the Challenge Cup final played at Wembley. I had no idea of the importance of this particular competition until we won the semi-final and the reaction of the players, staff and administrators of the club told me this was to be something big and special. In fact I almost cost us the opportunity to go the final after I threw a late wild pass which was picked up by the opposition and almost resulted in Hull Kingston Rovers scoring the winning try. Thankfully the player was pulled down short of the line and we hung on to win a place at Wembley.

The build up during the week leading up to the final was tremendous. There was excitement in the air and throughout the town of Wigan. Everywhere I went people would stop and talk about the final. I had played in Grand Finals for Parramatta, but this was a new experience for me. The club even fitted us out in new clothing, right down to new shoes. This was something I had never experienced before. It was really exciting. We travelled to London early in the week as part of out preparation and even snuck a training run on the hallowed Wembley turf before security removed us. It was an eerie feeling out in the middle with empty stands. But the view was breathtaking.

We had no sooner lined up for introductions on game day when I had already got myself offside with some people, who took me trying to remain calm and focused as being rude and disrespectful. I stood in line with my hands in the pockets of my Wigan jacket only because I didn't know what to do with them. Every time I was introduced to someone I shook their hand and put it back into my pocket. No disrespect was meant and I apologise to anyone who took offence. I couldn't believe all the storm of comment it had caused; that's British etiquette for you.

My fondest memory of the game was the try I scored; my first and only try on the famous Wembley soil. It came from a set play in which our scrum-half Michael Ford did a run around and then a pass across the face of our skipper Graeme West and hit me. I was able to run through the gap he'd created and into open field with only the Hull full-back Gary Kemble to beat. I started to look for our winger Henderson Gill, but I could not get a good sight of him. I thought to put my foot down and hope to be able to run around the full-back. As it was, he just hit my ankle with an attempted tackle, but I was able to keep my balance and score the try. It's nice to score tries, especially in finals, but this was extra special as it was at Wembley

Stadium. It's something I'll always be proud of and have it on tape to show my kids.

OTHER MEMORIES from the cup final include having a hand in our opening try. We were trailing 6-0 and I remember evading a number of Hull defenders before eventually offloading to loose-forward Ian Potter, who then sent Ferguson over in the corner. Gilly levelled the scores from the touchline. I also remember sending a smart ball out to David Stephenson, who shipped it on to Gill to race over and score. I think one of the strange moments of the final was playing against my Parramatta and Australia team-mate Peter Sterling, who was playing scrum-half for Hull. It was weird because I had played alongside him for the Eels, Australia and New South Wales and now I was up against him in the biggest game of the English season.

The celebrations after the victory went on well into the night. The bus trip home to Wigan seemed to take for ever, I guess with everyone desperately wanting to get back there to share the win with the Wigan people. When we arrived at Central Park the players went straight to the boardroom and out onto the balcony overlooking the ground. Not a blade of grass could be seen because of the supporters on the ground. It was a sea of cherry and white. Julie and myself couldn't stay all day and enjoy the celebrations as we had to drive my parents back to the airport to fly back to Australia. The club were very generous in flying my parents over to watch the Challenge Cup live at Wembley. The problem we faced was trying to get out of the car park and through Wigan, as there were people and cars everywhere around Central Park. We ended up getting a police escort out of Wigan so we could get my parents to the airport on time. That week would go down as one of the most memorable weeks of my football career.

JULIE AND I enjoyed our stay at Wigan. The people were friendly and accepted us as their own. The lifestyle was different to what we were used to, but that's what made the stay enjoyable. Julie enjoyed the shopping, in particular the markets in Wigan, but also the variety of department stores. Being close to cities like Bolton and Manchester was handy for her as well. The weather was not what we were used to, but it made our stay in England very special. It was the only time we actually lived somewhere where it actually snowed on our house! Of course we had to go out to the back yard and build a snowman and take photos to show our family back home.

I got the opportunity to go to London for a few days so we acted like usual tourists, doing plenty of sightseeing. It was something special to be able to stand in front of Buckingham Palace and walk through Madam Tussauds instead of seeing them on TV or in the magazines. In hindsight I wish I had for asked for a little more time off to have a look around Europe. My attitude, though, was that ultimately Wigan were paying me to play rugby league football for them and not to be travelling around Europe having fun.

While I enjoyed playing with Wigan and Julie and I made plenty of friends there, I was only signed to the club for the 1984/85 season, which ended in May '85, so that's why I had to leave. Also I still had commitments with Parramatta. There were, however, reports in some papers here in Australia and in England saying that my wife had our bags packed and was waiting for me outside the gates of the ground which we played the last game against St Helens, so when the game finished we could leave for Australia. That, of course, was not true and I did take legal action against the papers. We actually had two temporary bookings because that game against St Helens was a Premiership semi-final. If we won we would be leaving after the final a week later and if we lost we were booked to leave a few days after the game. I won't lie and say I wasn't looking forward to going home. When you've been away for a long period of time you do look forward to heading home even when you've had an enjoyable stay. But it wasn't the way some papers painted it.

People often ask me would I have gone back to play at Wigan or another club over in England. My honest answer has always been no. Financially it may have been better next time having played in and winning a Challenge Cup final, but that's the main reason I wouldn't go back. You see I had achieved everything players in Australia want to achieve in England, so therefore it didn't matter who I played for. I didn't think I could have achieved any more or done any better than I did the 1984/85 season at Wigan. I'm the type of guy that once I've achieved something and I'm happy with what I've achieved I don't feel the need to do it again and this was the case with rugby league in England.

I still take an interest in what happens at Wigan both on and off the field. I watch the Super League on Fox Sports here in Australia. I've been coaching at Penrith and my assistant coach there was former Wigan player Nigel Wright. We often talked about Wigan and how poorly they were performing in the 2006 season while at training. In fact when Wigan announced they were looking for a new coach both Nigel and myself thought about applying for the job. Unfortunately we couldn't get our CVs to Wigan before they announced the signing of former Bradford coach Brian Noble, who is obviously a great appointment. You never know, one day I might find myself coaching at Wigan and I know Nigel would be keen to come over too. My wife Julie has said she would love to be able to take our kids back to experience life in England. So you never know in rugby league – watch this space.

SHAUN WANE

PROP-FORWARD 1981–1990

SIGNED   14 September 1981 from Wigan St Patricks amateur rugby league club

DEBUT   3 January 1982 versus Barrow

WIGAN CAREER   150 appearances, 11 tries

HONOURS   Lancashire Cup 1985/86, 1987/88, John Player Special 1985/86, 1986/87, 1988/89, League Championship 1986/87, 1989/90, Premiership Trophy 1986/87, Challenge Cup 1987/88, World Club Challenge 1987, Regal Trophy 1989/90, Charity Shield 1987/88

LEFT   19 September 1990 to join Leeds a month after he played his final game for Wigan in a Charity Shield defeat against Widnes at the Vetch Field in Swansea

I THINK a lot of people were surprised when I mentioned I had recruited Shaun Wane to be a part of this book. I do not know why – I think people must forget that Shaun Wane is a Wigan lad; he played his amateur rugby league in the borough before signing for his home-town club and ran his blood to water for the best part of a decade.

Yes I agree Shaun Wane may not be the first name you automatically think of when you are making a list of your all-time Wigan greats, but he was a battler, a real hard worker and never let anyone down.

Wane is still involved at the club to this day. In 2007, he is the U18 coach and is doing a fine job helping to nurture the possible Shaun Edwards's, Andy Gregory's, Joe Lydon's and Shaun Wane's of the future.

WEDNESDAY 17th October 1987 was a memorable night in the history of English rugby league. This was the night when Wigan rugby league club became the first English club to beat Australian opposition in the World Club Challenge and set a precedent for other clubs to try and achieve even 20 years later.

During this chapter Shaun Wane looks back at that historical night with fond memories and explains how he did not let the 'sledging' from his opponents bother him and used up all his aggression to put in a fantastic performance which earned him the Man-of-the-Match award.

Also Wane explains what it is like for a Wigan-born youngster to get the opportunity to represent his home-town club and how it is an incredible feeling which is hard to put into words.

Wigan 8 v Manly-Warringah 2

World Club Challenge
Wednesday 7 October 1987

Central Park
Attendance 36,895

Teams

Steve Hampson	1	Dale Shearer
Richard Russell	2	David Ronson
David Stephenson	3	Darrell Williams
Joe Lydon	4	Michael O'Connor
Henderson Gill	5	Stuart Davies
Shaun Edwards	6	Cliff Lyons
Andy Gregory	7	Des Hasler
Brian Case	8	Phil Daley
Nicky Kiss	9	Mal Cochrane
Shaun Wane	10	Ian Gately
Andy Goodway	11	Ron Gibbs
Ian Potter	12	Owen Cunningham
Ellery Hanley	13	Paul Vautin
	Substitutes	
Ian Lucas	14	Paul Shaw
Ged Byrne	15	Jeremy Ticehurst
Graeme West	16	Mark Brokenshire
Ian Gildart	17	Mark Pocock
Stephenson 4	**Goals**	O'Connor

Referee: J Holdsworth

WITHOUT A doubt the best and the biggest game I have ever played in was the World Club Challenge game featuring Wigan and Manly in 1987. We beat them 8-2 and it was a fantastic feeling because nobody had given us a chance to win it, and to become the first team to actually win one of these matches was unbelievable.

It was the first ever World Club Challenge to be staged over here and our coach at the time Graham Lowe made sure we were fully focused on our job. We'd played a big game the weekend before. It was against our arch-rivals St Helens and then we played the Australian champions Manly on the Wednesday, plus we also had to play the Lancashire Cup final on the following Sunday, so we really had a very hectic schedule.

Before a game Graham Lowe would normally go easy on us in training, especially after so many matches in such a short period of time. He'd make sure we went through the motions, but nothing too strenuous. But what Graham did on the Monday and Tuesday before that Manly game was totally out of character – he had us doing full-contact training, so were absolutely knocking seven bells out of each other! There were split lips and broken teeth all flying about and that was in training. Graham had us fronting up that way because he was fully aware that this is what the game against Manly was going to be like and at the time I remember certain players thinking he was finally going a little bit mad, but to his credit it certainly paid off because in the game itself we didn't half rip in to them. So looking back we were lucky we had such a rigorous training session to prepare us. That is what made Graham Lowe such a great coach – he knew what we were up against and he knew how to get the best out of everyone, even if it meant almost killing each other in training. Now 20 years later it's still seems a mad way to prepare like that, but you can't complain because we created history.

I remember Graham not really saying much in the pre-match build up because he just let the atmosphere filter through and when we were sat in the dressing room you could smell all the pre-match fireworks going off and you could hear the buzz of a massive crowd outside which sounded different to all the other games we had played in at Central Park. It was a really, really vocal crowd and Lowe just allowed us to soak up the atmosphere by keeping quiet and it obviously paid off because we won. Once again that showed what a great coach Graham Lowe was and the team we had to be honest. He did not need to rant and rave to get us psyched up. He knew we were motivated, he just helped us along. It is small things like that that you remember about a coach and also the little things that make a great coach.

As kick-off time approached Graham told us he did not want us to run out on to the field, he wanted us to just remain calm and walk out in single file. That has to be one of the hardest things I have ever had to do if I am being honest with you. My nerves in my gut were jumping out my skin. I was trying my best to stay relaxed and just focus on the task in hand and throw a few a glances towards the Manly players in an attempt to try and out-psyche them. As we were walking out of the tunnel they were being very abusive towards our lads, you know, really bagging us like "You pommie this, pommie that, we're going to rip your f-ing heads off." To be fair that did not intimidate us, we just decided to fire some insults back at them and then after all the fireworks had been let off it was time for the real fireworks to begin. That was on the pitch and it was a real hard fought classic encounter.

THE FIRST time I looked at the clock, you know normally you look at the clock before half-time and see how long is left, there were two minutes left of the whole game – it went that fast. It was just a really, really quick game in all honesty. I just remember the first two tackles. I gave away a couple of penalties for high tackles which was quite surprising because the bloke who I did the high tackles on was 6ft 5ins and I am only 5ft 11ins. It was just one of those sorts of games which you just sprung into the tackles as hard as you could and hit them with everything you could and that's the way it was. So I suppose with the intensity of the occasion there were always going to be a few reckless challenges.

Even though we played so many tough games around that time I just did not feel tired at all, it was all just adrenalin. I was running on that adrenalin and now knowing there was only two minutes left it was even more important to keep going. With me being a Wigan born lad, it was more special to me because it meant so much to our town folk.

LOOKING BACK at the game it was a very bruising clash and definitely a forwards battle – I think that proved itself with me getting the Man-of-the-Match award. I just tried to play my natural game, which was to defend solid and take the ball up with real venom, and it paid off. But it was certainly a team effort and I am still very proud I got the chance to play in that wonderful game.

It was unbelievable. There were just under 37,000 people crammed into Central Park to see us play. We did not get off to the best possible start when the referee John Holdsworth penalised us, I think it was for off-side, and Australian Test centre Michael O'Connor, who later played for St Helens, slotted over the penalty to give them a 2-0 lead.

We soon got back in the game when we were awarded a penalty ourselves after an incident involving myself and Des Hasler. Our centre David Stephenson levelled the scores with that penalty and then extended our lead to 4-2 when he converted another penalty after Dale Shearer was penalised after a bust-up with Shaun Edwards. We took that slender lead into the half-time break.

Seconds after the break Mal Cochrane committed a foul on Edwards and Stephenson slotted over the resulting penalty. He then added his fourth and final kick of the night when Manly second-row forward Ron Gibbs was sent off for a late challenge on Joe Lydon as he attempted a drop-goal. This made the score 8-2 and we hung on for those last few, long minutes to claim the victory. As I said, it was a fierce battle and for both teams not to concede any tries was a credit to the defences. Both sides had chances but no-one could manage to get over the whitewash.

I was never one for showing much emotion when I first scored a try, got man of the match or anything like that, but when that final whistle went I remember just jumping in the air and hugging Ellery Hanley. He was pretty similar to me at showing emotion i.e. he never showed any, but he was so excited and it was such a relief. It was unbelievable! The best feeling ever! We were all just celebrating; it was such a massive game and I know I'd never been like that before. The reason we were so excited was the pressure we'd felt and absolutely nobody had given us a chance to win the game against a great Manly team. It made it even more special because of the grief we got off the Manly players before and during the game.

As a rugby league player you do not like to get injured, but when you do you always want to play on and most players need to be dragged off that pitch, get patched up and back on as soon as the coach lets you, but the Manly lads that night did not seem to want to play on once they got injured. So that was another battle won, I suppose. You never want to show the opposition you are hurting, but Manly did that night and it spurred us on to victory – it was just a fantastic feeling, you know.

It was a World Club Challenge match and I found it insulting that the fans had paid good money to watch such a special team as Manly, who had won the Australian Grand Final, then their players chose to behave like this; also before the game to find out that they were to rest some key players. For me, as a coach, you make sure that you field the best team possibly on that day no matter what the game or the opposition. I was just glad that they did not have the excuse of injured players or being able to say if the players that had not played that night had played they would have won. They had no excuses. We beat their best team that night and that's a fact!

There were no foreigners in the Wigan team that night. We were all English and that made it even better that an English team had beaten the best Australian team at that time. There were Wigan born and bred lads in the team such as Shaun Edwards as well as myself which in itself it made the win twice as nice. A win like that means more to the likes of me and Shaun than the other lads who did not know as much of the history of Wigan. One instance of this that stands out in my mind and I think explains it nicely is Dean Bell's first game for the club. It was Leigh away at Hilton Park and any Wiganer knows the rivalry there. As the final whistle went, the score board showed Leigh 0 visitors 30. Shaun Edwards and I were jumping around the pitch celebrating as if we had just won the Challenge Cup at Wembley while Dean just walked off the pitch happy that another game had been won to gain the two points. It was a local derby and you cannot really explain the way it feels to play for your home-town club and to nil your rivals. Even the players with the stature of Ellery Hanley could not understand why were so excited. He even said that he could not understand why we were so proud to play for Wigan and that we thought we were better than anybody else because we came from Wigan. I think he got the same feelings eventually and understands why were so happy to win games against teams like Leigh and St Helens.

It's bred into you when you're from Wigan from an early age! No amount of talent can make up for that in some situations!

As I said earlier you do not like to miss games, I have been unfortunate to miss a number of key matches in my career. Whether it be squad rotation, injuries or even suspension – no matter how you miss a game it always hurts. I missed a couple of Challenge Cup finals, which is still hard to take because of the history of the tournament. One was through suspension and that was really tough – I was suspended for six games. I was in control of my destiny and that's what upset me more than anything else. It was my own emotion what made me get banned and it is something I could control, but when I got injured for another Challenge Cup final, there was not much I can do. For the suspended game I went down to London with the team and it was heartbreaking, you know, to see all the Wigan fans and I just wanted to be a part of the game and physically get stuck in and be with the lads after the game, but it just never feels the same no matter how much they try to involve you, it is never the same.

Wembley is a fantastic place, I did manage to appear there for the club as a substitute against Halifax in 1988 – it was a brilliant feeling, I only got on for the last couple of minutes, but that did not matter, just to be out on the field was amazing.

I think one of the Cup finals I missed was against St Helens in 1989 when we beat them 27-0. It's bred into you when you're from Wigan that that is the ultimate. It is unbelievable to go to Wembley and beat them like we did, and it was a great feeling. I was happy for the lads in one sense, but in a selfish sort of way I was upset for myself that I was not part of it. I missed two Challenge Cup finals through suspension and two with injuries, but being honest with you I don't want to remember them – not when there are so many great memories to relive... over and over again.

ANDY GREGORY

SCRUM-HALF 1987–1992

SIGNED   From Warrington in 1987

DEBUT   18 January 1987 versus Workington Town

WIGAN CAREER   182 appearances, 17 tries, 28 goals (including six drop goals)

HONOURS   World Club Championship 1987, 1991 Rugby League Championship 1986/87, 1989/90, 1990/91, 1991/92 Challenge Cup 1988, 1989, 1990, 1991, 1992 Premiership Trophy 1987 John Player Special/Regal Trophy 1988/89, 1989/90 Lancashire Cup 1987, 1988 Charity Shield 1987, 1991 Great Britain Tourist 1988, 1992 Lancashire Representative honours

LEFT   His final match for Wigan was in the 1992 Challenge Cup final against Castleford in 1992 – he went off injured at half time. He joined Leeds after his spell at Wigan before going to Salford where he eventually became head coach

ANDY GREGORY will go down in history as one of the greatest scrum-halves not only just to play for Wigan, but to play the game of rugby league. Gregory could change the tempo of any game and was the catalyst of many of Wigan's greatest victories.

Gregory joined the club from Warrington after spending a few years at Widnes where he appeared in three Challenge Cup finals, so when he arrived at Central Park he was a already well known star and keen to add to his silverware collection. Gregory formed a formidable partnership with stand-off Shaun Edwards which struck fear into every club side in England and eventually Australia – The little general collected a staggering 18 trophies during his five-year spell – a quite remarkable achievement and he still boasts the proud record of never being on the losing side at Wembley.

Having watched all of Gregory's career in a Wigan shirt a number of incidents stand out in my mind. The first one was missing a conversion virtually in front of the posts during the 1988 Challenge Cup final against Halifax; secondly the cheeky drop goal that made it 13-0 in our fantastic 27-0 rout over St Helens at Wembley in 1989. There was another incident during a Wigan versus Widnes clash at Naughton Park where Gregory was dismissed from the field after the referee adjudged that he had bitten the hand of Widnes enforcer Kurt Sorensen – I think what made the occasion more memorable is that Gregory would hardly have been able to get his mouth around Sorensen's hand, it was that big.

One final incident involving Gregory is probably in the top 10 of most fans' memorable moments in rugby league. Picture the scene; it's the third Test, Australia v Great Britain in 1988 with a few minutes remaining. Gregory gets the ball about five yards from his own line, he evades a couple of high shots before sending loose-forward Mike Gregory, who later became Wigan coach, racing away to score with Wayne Pearce chasing in vain. The best part of the try was watching arguably the fastest winger in the world at that time – Martin Offiah – trying to keep up with Mike Gregory only to have his shirt pulled back by Australia stand-off Wally Lewis. After the try the camera showed a shot of Andy Gregory and he looked delighted and shattered, by the look on his face you though he had just run 85 yards not 15 or 20. He gave his all for both club and country.

ANDY GREGORY'S love affair with Wembley started well before his career with Wigan even looked like beginning. Gregory made his Twin Towers debut back in 1981 for Widnes, and made two more appearances at the famous ground for the Chemics before finally getting the opportunity to walk out at Wembley for his home town club. That year was 1988 – just 12 months after he joined the famous cherry and whites from his second club Warrington.

In this chapter Gregory talks about what it was like playing for Wigan in that 1988 Challenge Cup final at Wembley and the feeling he got when he was chosen as the Lance Todd Trophy winner for most outstanding player after 80 minutes.

As well as the 1988 final, Gregory also passes comment on a number of other Challenge Cup final victories which include the 27–0 win over St Helens in 1989 and how he still infuriates Saints fans who are haunted by that game with his little quirky remarks.

Gregory also reveals how he also came to blows with one of his friends while he was playing for Widnes against Wigan and remembers his final ever game in a Wigan shirt, which very aptly ended at yes, you guessed it – Wembley.

Wigan 32 v Halifax 12

Challenge Cup final
Saturday 30 April 1988

Wembley Stadium
Attendance 94,273

Teams

Joe Lydon	1	Graham Eadie
Tony Iro	2	Martin Meredith
Kevin Iro	3	Chris Anderson
Dean Bell	4	Ian Wilkinson
Henderson Gill	5	Colin Whitfield
Shaun Edwards	6	Bob Grogan
Andy Gregory	7	Steve Robinson
Brian Case	8	Neil James
Nicky Kiss	9	Seamus McCallion
Adrian Shelford	10	Keith Neller
Andy Goodway	11	Les Holiday
Ian Potter	12	Paul Dixon
Ellery Hanley	13	John Pendlebury
Substitutes		
Ged Byrne	14	Mick Scott
Shaun Wane	15	Dick Fairbank
K Iro 2, Gill, Lydon T Iro, Hanley, Bell	**Tries**	Anderson, James
Gregory, Lydon	**Goals**	Whitfield 2

Referee: F Lindop

AS EVERYONE knows I am a Wigan lad and I was fortunate to play for the club for six seasons, so really any game I played wearing the famous cherry and white will always remain special and close to my heart.

I suppose one of my favourite games in a Wigan shirt, though, has to be the 1988 Challenge Cup final against the holders Halifax at Wembley. The Challenge Cup is such a momentous occasion and I have been very fortunate to have played in so many cup finals for both Widnes and Wigan, but to actually walk out at the Twin Towers in front of thousands of people for your home-town club is something I will never forget and will treasure for years to come.

IN 1988 I was very fortunate to play in such a very good Wigan side – the players we had like, Shaun Edwards, Ellery Hanley, Kevin and Tony Iro, Joe Lydon, Graeme West and Dean Bell where all match winners in their own right. It was a joy to play with players like that. Looking back and being honest with you I think we would have beaten any team in the world on that day

Also in that final at Wembley against Halifax I was lucky enough to win the Lance Todd Trophy award as the press believed I was the best player on the park. I've got to say I won the Lance Todd Trophy on two occasions while wearing a Wigan shirt. The second was against Warrington two years later in 1990, but to win it for the first time in my first Challenge Cup final appearance with my home-town club was absolutely marvellous. It does not get much better than that really. We prepared well for the game all week, we did a good and proper professional job and we basically did what we set out to do and that was to return back to Wigan with the Challenge Cup.

My first Wembley Challenge Cup final had been in 1981 when I played for Widnes against Hull Kingston Rovers, which was a very proud moment for me. Even though it was not for Wigan, I still look back at that moment, I was only a young kid and it was my Wembley debut. I managed to score a try as well after collecting a ball from Mick Adams to win 18-9. That was a fine start to my relationship with Wembley.

The year after Widnes played Hull and we drew 14-14 before finally conceding defeat in a replay 19-6 at Elland Road in Leeds. What was funny was that in 1984 myself and Joe Lydon, who were Wigan born lads, were in the Widnes side that inflicted defeat on Wigan in the Challenge Cup final. The funny feeling was playing in a Challenge Cup final – which is regarded as one of the major cup competitions in the world – against the town and the club where I was born. It was just strange being a Wiganer, but doing my utmost to ensure Wigan lost the game, which I did. Widnes were too strong and quick for Wigan that day and Joe Lydon was just unstoppable, I think Wigan knew that because they eventually signed us both up.

One of my best mates, Graeme West – who I played with many times in a cherry and white shirt and I am still very close to today – was up against me that me day and we ended up in a brawl with each other. I am five foot four and he's six foot four, so I suppose that was a hilarious sight for the fans to see me swinging arms upwards and him bending down to try and smack me one.

Against Halifax we were so focused on just doing the job and bringing home some more silverware for the supporters. I knew on the Wednesday leading up to the game on the Saturday that we were going to win the Challenge Cup. The preparation was just spot-on, full credit to the coaching staff they worked their socks off getting us match ready, but deep down I knew there was no way we would lose this game. I do not think I was being cocky or arrogant, but I just had full confidence in my own ability and my team-mates that we would brush Halifax aside and come home with the cup.

We had a team full of international players; if you dropped the ball in training you got a severe rollicking as if you drop a ball in training you might take that mindset into a game situation and that was not acceptable for a club like Wigan. It was just work, work, work all week long at Test match pace. Those were the standards we set and we always wanted to improve on that no matter what the occasion and no matter who the opponents were.

THIS MAY sound a bit daft, but I am totally serious, on that day against Halifax I honestly believe if Wigan had been playing the Australian Test team we would have walked off the field victorious. Considering the preparation we went through I honestly believe we would have beaten them. I am not being disrespectful to the Aussies because they had some great players at the time including Wally Lewis, Mal Meninga, Peter Sterling and Paul Vautin, but with the calibre of stars we had in that squad and under the guidance of coach Graham Lowe I do think we would have turned them over.

I had already played at Wembley three times before for Widnes and I had played in World Club Championships, Test matches and games like that, but as a Wigan lad in front of your family to be awarded the Lance Todd Trophy is something very special and something you treasure for ever. I really mean that you cannot really put it into words what winning that trophy means to a player. I was extremely lucky because I won it again against Warrington in 1990.

Wembley is just a fantastic place to be able to play rugby league. I remember in 1981 when I went with my brother – our Bryn – he got a ticket to come down and watch me with all my family and I could not for the life of me tell him what it was like to play on such a big occasion. It was just a blur to me. He kept going on at me "Andy, what was it like?" And I just had to reply "Bryn, I am going to have to go back again because I cannot remember one little thing that happened." At the time I do not think anyone of us would believe I would return to Wembley another eight times after that.

HALIFAX MADE quite a decent start and it was more of a forwards' battle during the opening 20 minutes, but once we crossed for that first try there was no stopping us really. I remember making a half break before sending Shaun Edwards steaming through a gap. He was brought down inches from the line and at the resulting play-the-ball our massive New Zealand international centre Kevin Iro forced his way over. Kevin was hard to stop anyway, but from two yards you basically had no chance. Four minutes later I think I made another break before offloading to Dean Bell who eventually sent Henderson Gill over in the corner. Kevin Iro then added his second try of the afternoon before I once again created another try for Joe Lydon to score in a move that involved Shaun Edwards, Henderson Gill and Dean Bell. We went in at the break leading 16-0. Being honest I think we know it would take a tremendous effort from Halifax to fight back for a Wigan, so we were determined not to ease up.

We basically started the second half in the way we finished the first by scoring straight away. Tony Iro, Kevin's brother, collected one of my long balls to cross over in the corner to extend our lead to 20-0. Straight from the restart the ball went to our full-back Joe Lydon, who then ran about 70 yards untouched before handing the ball onto Ellery Hanley, who evaded the clutches of Halifax winger Martin Meredith, to score under the sticks. At 26-0 there was no way we going to buckle – the Challenge Cup was coming back to Wigan.

I later went through another gap before sending Dean Bell through to score a final try which was sandwiched in the middle of two consolation scores for Halifax by Chris Anderson and Neil James. We won the game 32-12. In all fairness to Halifax, who were a very good side, we were just too good for them on the day.

THE 1989 Challenge Cup final victory over St Helens was special as well. It is a local derby isn't it? There is a lot of pride at stake and a whole lot of bragging rights to be earned. At the moment they are one of the best teams around in world rugby, but they never ever beat me at Wembley. I played against Saints twice there, but the first one when we hammered them 27-0 in 1989 was brilliant. I love seeing St Helens with no points and I also love seeing Wigan walking off with the Cup.

We got off to a wonderful start. Joe Lydon put a high bomb to test their young full-back Gary Connoll., I think he was only 17 or something like that at the time. He knocked-on and a few moments later Ellery Hanley went on a surging run before offloading to Kevin Iro, whose brute strength got him over the try line. I think that try calmed everyone down a little, but despite a penalty from Joe Lydon, it took us another 20 minutes before we crossed over again. Hanley took the ball from a Shaun Edwards pass to skip pass a handful of Saints defenders to send us into the half-time break leading 12-0.

Within a few minutes after the break I slotted over a cheeky drop-goal which hurt St Helens to give us a 13-0 lead. I think that really ended their challenge that day. Kevin Iro then forced his way over for his second try of the afternoon before Shaun Edwards broke through the St Helens defence to throw me a pass to stroll in under the posts – that was a very good feeling. With just a couple of minutes remaining we ended Saints' misery when full-back Steve Hampson, who had missed Wigan's last three Wembley appearances through injury, collected an unselfish ball from Joe Lydon to score our final try to make the score 27-0 and another Challenge Cup final win for Wigan.

IT IS great for me when I do some after-match speaking in St Helens. I always get people asking me about my career and I always tell them one of my special moments was when Wigan beat St Helens 28-0 at Wembley in the Challenge Cup final in 1989 – they automatically shout out "but it was 27-0 Andy!" "That's my problem,.' I reply. "I always seem to get Wigan's score wrong, but I always get Saints' score right!"

That Challenge Cup run of five consecutive victories will always be special to me. We just seemed to be unstoppable at Wembley, and it was a great feeling. In 1990 we played a very good Warrington side, but our fitness and skill was too much for them, I think Kevin Iro got a try double for the third consecutive year a remarkable feat in itself and we ran out comfortable 36-14 winners and I managed to collect my second Lance Todd Trophy award. Then in 1991 we got another win over St Helens 13–8. It was a lot closer than in 1989, but a special win all the same because it is always good to beat the old enemy.

The Challenge Cup final victory over Castleford in 1992 was not only my last Wembley appearance for Wigan it was actually my last ever appearance in a Wigan shirt. I got injured and was taken off at half-time and I never played for the club again. We got off to another good start at Wembley when Martin Offiah followed up his own kick to beat Graham Steadman to score the first try. Further tries in the first half from Shaun Edwards and Martin Offiah followed by three Frano Botica goals and a Joe Lydon drop-goal saw us lead 19-0 at half-time. Unfortunately I played no further part as we eventually defeated Castleford 28-12, with Steve Hampson crossing for a try, two Botica goals and another Lydon drop-goal. It was a very sad way to end my career at Central Park, but I had some great times and I was very proud every time I got the chance to wear the famous cherry and white and I still go and watch them at the JJB Stadium and hope we can get back to winning ways very soon.

IN THE past few years it has been disappointing watching Wigan and the 2006 season where we just avoided relegation was hard to stomach considering the history surrounding the club. Even though I am a Wigan lad I also love my rugby league and I always like the sport doing well – so I can honestly say I was delighted when St Helens won the BBC Sports Personality Team of the Year in 2006.

But Wigan in the next few seasons will be back on form. I am not saying they will necessarily win anything, but we will have better years than when almost went down. Things are looking really bright for the future of Wigan rugby league club.

DEAN BELL

CENTRE 1986–1994

SIGNED From Eastern Suburbs (Australia) in September 1986

DEBUT 7 September 1986 v Leigh

WIGAN CAREER 253 appearances, 96 tries

HONOURS Rugby League Championship 1986/87, 1989/90, 1990/91, 1991/92, 1992/93, 1993/94, Challenge Cup 1988, 1989, 1990, 1991, 1992, 1993, 1994, Premiership Trophy 1987, 1992, John Player Special/Regal Trophy 1986/87, 1988/89, 1989/90, 1992/93, Lancashire Cup 1986, 1987, 1988, 1992, Charity Shield 1987, 1991. New Zealand tourist 1985, 1986, 1987 (captain), New Zealand, New Zealand Maoris, Auckland, South Island, Cumbria

LEFT Joined former coach John Monie at the newly former Auckland Warriors in their inaugural season in Australia in 1995

DEAN BELL has been an iconic figure for Wigan on and off the field for the past 20 years. The New Zealand centre arrived in Wigan in 1986 from Australian club side Eastern Suburbs after brief spells in England with Carlisle and Leeds. Straight away Bell became a firm fans' favourite with his no-nonsense tackling style which eventually earned him the moniker 'Mean Dean'.

Dean appeared in seven Wembley Challenge Cup finals from 1988-1994 and was never on the losing side, captaining the team on three occasions. He won the much coveted Lance Todd Trophy award for Man-of-the-Match in the 1993 final victory over Widnes, when he assumed the loose-forward role instead of his normal centre position.

During his time at the club, Wigan featured in three World Club Challenges, winning two. Unfortunately due to injury Dean only played in one of them – this was the 1992 defeat to Brisbane Broncos at Central Park.

Dean also scooped the 1992 Man Of Steel award, which is presented to the player deemed to have had the most impact at club level during that season. In 1993 he was paid a surprise visit by TV presenter Michael Aspel on the pitch after a game against Leeds. Aspel uttered those famous word which will never be forgotten by any Wigan fan: "Dean Bell – This is Your Life".

Dean's last appearance in the famous cherry and white was the 1994 Challenge Cup final against Leeds, as he departed back to New Zealand to team up with former Wigan coach John Monie at the newly formed Auckland Warriors. He later returned to England as coach of Leeds before eventually making his way back to Wigan as Rugby Executive, overseeing all areas of youth development including the Under 21s, Under 18s and the scholarship scheme. Dean left again in February 2007 and was then inducted into Wigan rugby league club's Hall of Fame.

HALIFAX WERE the holders of the Challenge Cup following their victory over St Helens twelve months earlier and I suppose could have been dubbed as favorites as it was Wigan's first visit to the Twin Towers since their 1985 success against Hull. Halifax had a number of quality players in their line-up with Graham Eadie, Les Holiday, Paul Dixon and former Central Park favourite John Pendlebury, but Wigan were not there just to make up the numbers and boasted a field of talented superstars included young captain Shaun Edwards, Ellery Hanley, Bell himself and Andy Gregory.

Wigan 32 v Halifax 12

Challenge Cup final
Saturday 30 April 1988

Wembley Stadium
Attendance 94,273

Teams

Wigan		Halifax
Joe Lydon	1	Graham Eadie
Tony Iro	2	Martin Meredith
Kevin Iro	3	Chris Anderson
Dean Bell	4	Ian Wilkinson
Henderson Gill	5	Colin Whitfield
Shaun Edwards	6	Bob Grogan
Andy Gregory	7	Steve Robinson
Brian Case	8	Neil James
Nicky Kiss	9	Seamus McCallion
Adrian Shelford	10	Keith Neller
Andy Goodway	11	Les Holiday
Ian Potter	12	Paul Dixon
Ellery Hanley	13	John Pendlebury
Substitutes		
Ged Byrne	14	Mick Scott
Shaun Wane	15	Dick Fairbank
K Iro 2, Gill, Lydon T Iro, Hanley, Bell	**Tries**	Anderson, James
Gregory, Lydon	**Goals**	Whitfield 2

Referee: F Lindop

LOOKING BACK it is quite difficult to choose one specific game as my best ever in a Wigan shirt because I had so many throughout my career. I was very fortunate in that regard. But I think one of the games that first comes to mind really is the Challenge Cup final at Wembley in 1988 against Halifax.

The thing about it was just going into the unknown really. As a youngster when I was six or seven growing up in New Zealand I remember getting up in the early hours of the morning turning on the TV to watch the Challenge Cup final. Like any young kid it was my dream to play at such a great venue – and probably not for any moment in a little day dream did I ever think it would be possible.

AFTER WE finally won the semi-final against Salford, obviously I had to keep fit and stay in form to get selected, but we were all focused on the final and it felt like virtually stepping into the unknown for most of the players.

I do remember visiting the stadium for the first time the day before the game and I did spend quite a bit of time on my own actually going up into the seats and just absorbing the whole place because it was such a magnificent stadium. It probably did not really prepare me for what would happen on the day, but it was a time just to gather my thoughts and think about performing really. That was the main thing, you know. I was very anxious about playing as well as I could in the game. It is alright going into such a big final and reaching your goals and dreams and that, but it is important that you play to the best of your ability while you are there.

The day of the game – I remember sort of being an hour away from the ground at the hotel and getting on the bus, but the closer we got to the stadium the more people we would see spilling out of pubs and places. Seeing that really started to get the old nerves going and the heartbeat racing and when we finally got to Wembley Way – because the bus used to go down Wembley Way in those days – the bus driver stopped and Graham Lowe, the coach of Wigan at the time, put the theme tune to the Rocky movie on and I remember just going through those thousands of people with that music blaring out in my ears. It was just so good. The adrenaline was rushing through my body and I remember as we got to the gate, because you had to slow down and park in the tunnel area, I could see young kids sat on their grandfathers' shoulders and you could really see what it meant to the fans. It was very, very inspiring and really motivated me to believe that I actually had the chance to be a part of something that could bring real pleasure to so many people.

Preparation in the changing rooms is just like any other game to be honest with you. You prepare the same way, but obviously you know that it is not just a normal game going out there. I always hear people say: "it's just like any other game," but it's not really – there are millions of people watching it all over the world, there are a hundred thousand people watching in the stadium and you put yourself up there to be criticised or praised, so it is important that you go out there and do not freeze.

It is something that we talked about as a team the night before as well. At that time it was certainly the biggest game I had ever played in, I had never been in front of a crowd like that. I had played in Test matches for New Zealand, but I think the biggest crowd would have been 46,000. I had never played in a stadium like Wembley before and it was just the aura of the place – with so much history – that made it so special. You just had to get ready as normal.

You have to wait in the tunnel area – and then we got the nod from the BBC, so it was a nervous time in the tunnel because you have to stand next to your opposition guy who you will be marking because you all walk out in number order apart from the captain. We also talked the night before about remaining focused and not forgetting the reason why we were there and that was to win a game of rugby league. So it was valuable to remain focused and it is what I have always said when you are in huge situations like that – you play the game, not the occasion.

I could hear the noise of the crowd in the background, but you couldn't really make out what was going on. It was just sort of a blur really. It was not until we got the ok from the BBC guys to walk out that we knew what was really happening. As soon as I went past the covered area of the tunnel the explosion of noise and colour just hit me – and I must admit I had goose pimples all over my body. When I got to the halfway line to meet the dignitaries it was like my feet were not even touching the ground. It was quite an unbelievable feeling really.

After that it was all about why we were there and what we had to do. I remember many of the Halifax players had been there the previous year against St Helens and had won. I do not know whether they were relaxed because of that or whatever, but I saw them waving away to their wives, girlfriends and family members and all that, whereas we were really focused and concentrating on what we were there for and that was to win the Challenge Cup.

THE GAME itself was quite special. We played really well. I remember coming on to a short ball from our scrum-half Andy Gregory and then I threw a long ball out to our winger Henderson Gill, who went to score in the corner before giving us his trademark smile as he lay on the ground – and a little dance as well, if I remember correctly. Gill's try came after Kevin Iro had opened the scoring. It had been a tight affair in the opening 25 minutes until Andy Gregory sent Shaun Edwards through a gap and Shaun was brought down inches short. Iro then forced his way over. I think Joe Lydon scored a try in a move where I was involved. It was a very slick passing movement and Joe went over after taking the final pass off me.

In the second-half I recall Ellery Hanley scoring a try that only he could score; taking a pass from Lydon before moving sideways like a crab, evading a number of defenders, before putting the ball down under the posts. I remember grabbing a try myself – it was something I wanted to do, you know, just to say I had scored a try at Wembley. Ellery had made a break and the cover defence was coming across to close him down, so he threw a ball over the top of the defender. The ball bounced on the ground and I just picked it up on the run. The covering defender approached me, so I pushed him off and went over by the right side of the posts. It was certainly a nice feeling to score at Wembley, I think everybody would like to do that in any big game and then afterwards it was relief more than anything that we had played well and won the game.

When the game was over I walked up the steps towards the Royal Box thinking about how privileged I was and about how many famous people in all walks of sport who have had the chance to do that in whose footsteps I was following and, to be fair, the many thousands who hadn't had the chance to do that. So I thought: "if my career finishes tomorrow, at least I have achieved this." There was no way in the world that I thought that I would return to Wembley another six times and win them all.

I NEVER took any of those Challenge Cup finals for granted because each time we went to Wembley was a privilege and each time we thought, "this could be our last time," so we gave respect to the event and the game and also to make sure we did our best when we were out there. No-one ever wanted to go out there and freeze on the big occasion. Obviously the more times we went to Wembley we knew what to expect. The second time was going into the known; totally different from the previous year. It didn't have that same effect. It didn't have the surprise element, but the occasion itself was fantastic and to do it nearly every season I was at the club was a tremendous achievement really. I never lost respect for the Challenge Cup. I knew what history laid behind it all and we didn't really think about how we were writing ourselves into the record books; it was just a case of playing well and peaking at the right time each time we played in the tournament.

The bonus that goes with winning a Challenge Cup final is the homecoming – you never forget those. We actually do have reason to forget most of them regarding the alcohol we drank! They were quite surreal occasions being honest with you. You could not believe that so many people would turn up to welcome us home to Wigan. I think back now and I cannot believe the commitment of some of the supporters and what they had done to their houses, the banners they made and the effort they had put in to us arriving back from Wembley. It was very special to me. After experiencing it the first time after we beat Halifax in a lot of ways that's what sort of inspired me to do well at Wembley again in the Challenge Cup because that was the part I really, really looked forward to the most – the homecomings.

I remember in 1987 Oldham beat us in the Challenge Cup – they went down in history as the last team that beat us before that glorious run. That defeat taught us a valuable lesson about not taking anything for granted. We knew we had a really good team together and I honestly thought we had a good chance of getting to Wembley that year, so when we turned up on that awful night at the Watersheddings maybe we were complacent and we rightly got beaten. That gave us a kick up the backside we needed and from then on we did not take anything for granted and that was possibly the catalyst for that record-breaking winning run. So in 1988 we were fired up because of the previous year when Oldham had knocked us out. I think that was the only trophy we didn't win that season, so everyone in the team was really keen to make up for that and add the Challenge Cup to our trophy cabinet. We were all so disappointed that we'd failed the year before, so, being honest, it was like we were obsessed to put things right.

WHEN WE beat Salford in the semi-final to reach the 1988 final there was huge relief around the club that we had finally got there, but then you had to make sure your form was good so you got selected plus you also had to stay fit and there were plenty of opposition players who would remind you in tackles between the semi and the final – a kind of polite 'be careful' message that you had to get past them in one piece before making the final. Well, that was like a red rag to a bull to me. It did not make any difference to the way I played the game. You play it one way and that is full out, no matter what is in front of you. Some players rest themselves a week before the final or whatever, but you just can't pick and choose the games you perform in. You have to take every game as it comes.

1988 was my second year at the club and I knew I was playing with a very special team. It was quite obvious that some of the players could do things you knew could win big games. And also the good thing about the team I was playing in was that they knew how to win the tough games as well. It wasn't just a case that we could perform on a nice sunny April/May day at Wembley on lovely turf, we could also turn up at places like Hull and Castleford. You could never just call us a good weather team because we could roll our sleeves up and play tough when we had to as well. It was an amazing array of talent that we had and I was very fortunate to be a part of that and I look back at my playing days at Wigan with very fond memories.

Another important occasion in my career was winning the Lance Todd Trophy against Widnes in 1993. The more times you go to the Challenge Cup final the more opportunities you have to win the Man of the Match award and I knew a little bit of history surrounding it. I knew, for example, that it was a Kiwi who it was named after. Anybody who plays in a final wants to get that Man of the Match award whether they say they do or they don't; surely they do and I was no different. I always knew it would be quite difficult for me to win while I was playing as a centre because we had so many quality players in positions that saw a lot more of the ball than I did, like Shaun Edwards, Andy Gregory and Ellery Hanley. So it was when I went to loose-forward that I actually won it and that was a great moment.

To have gone to Wembley seven times, I would have been a little bit annoyed with myself not to have won it once. I am not one who is really into Man of the Match trophies because they are about someone else's opinion and they are not always an accurate reflection of how well you have played during the game. I just knew the status that particular award held throughout the game. Every year I always turn up to the Lance Todd Trophy presentation in Salford because I respect the tradition of the event. I go along and meet the older players and some of the more recent stars. It is always a great night and it also great to see your name on that prestigious list.

BILLY McGINTY

SECOND ROW 1991–1994

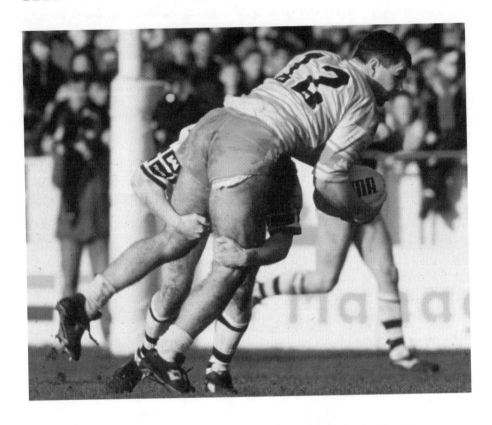

SIGNED Ahead of the 1991/92 season from local rivals Warrington

DEBUT 1 September 1991 v Castleford

WIGAN CAREER 75 appearances, 9 tries

HONOURS World Club Challenge 1991, 1994, Rugby league championship 1991/92, 1992/93, 1993/94, Challenge Cup 1992, Lancashire Cup 1992/93, Regal Trophy 1993

LEFT In 1994 after the World Club Challenge victory in Brisbane and eventually joined Workington Town

BILLY McGINTY was an unsung hero in his three seasons at Central Park. He arrived from Warrington having actually lined up against Wigan in the 1990 Challenge Cup final at Wembley. McGinty was your traditional hard-working second row forward. He never took a backward step and was always willing to help out with the hard yards.

His unique running style, coupled with his socks rolled down to his ankles, made him a firm favourite among the Central Park faithful, who truly appreciated his efforts. In his first season at the club, Billy won the World Club Challenge as Wigan defeated Australian champions Penrith Panthers at Anfield. He also walked off with the rugby league Championship trophy and the Challenge Cup. He was selected for the Great Britain Ashes Tour to Australia in 1992 and helped the team beat the Aussies in the second Test in Melbourne. That game was also special for the fact that the whole pack was provided by Wigan – a first ever for the national team. Billy lined up with his five team-mates Andy Platt, Kelvin Skerrett, Martin Dermott, Denis Betts and Phil Clarke.

Billy's last season in the famous cherry and white was not his best personally as he was hampered by injuries and only featured in four matches as well as five substitute appearances. However his final game for the club was in Brisbane at the ANZ Stadium for Wigan's historic World Club Challenge victory against the Broncos. He played in place of the injured Kelvin Skerrett and started at prop for the first time in his career to collect the coveted trophy for the second time himself and the third in Wigan's history.

Here McGinty recalls his career at Central Park and also his legendary run-in with Prime Minister John Major and how he was pestered by the national press for months later!

WIGAN HAD defeated Bradford Northern 71-10 in the semi-final at Burnden Park to make it through to their fourth consecutive Challenge Cup final appearance, winger Martin Offiah ran in five tries against the Yorkshire side and was favourite to become the first rugby league player in history to score three tries in a Wembley cup final – unfortunately he did not create history after his hat-trick was disallowed for a knock-on.

Wigan 28 v Castleford 12

Challenge Cup final
Saturday 2 May 1992

Wembley Stadium
Attendance 77,286

Teams

Joe Lydon	1	Graham Steadman
Frano Botica	2	Jon Wray
Dean Bell	3	St John Ellis
Gene Miles	4	Richie Blackmore
Martin Offiah	5	David Nelson
Shaun Edwards	6	Grant Anderson
Andy Gregory	7	Mike Ford
Kelvin Skerrett	8	Lee Crooks
Martin Dermott	9	Graham Southernwood
Andy Platt	10	Keith England
Denis Betts	11	Graham Bradley
Billy McGinty	12	Martin Ketteridge
Phil Clarke	13	Tawera Nikau
	Substitutes	
Steve Hampson	14	Tony Smith
Neil Cowie	15	Dean Sampson
Offiah 2, Edwards Hampson	**Tries**	Blackmore, England
Botica 5	**Goals**	Ketteridge 2

Referee: R Whitfield

WHEN I was at Warrington I always used to set myself little goals and ambitions with things you really want to achieve out of rugby. I desperately wanted to play for Great Britain, for example. Another of them goals was to play at Wembley. A couple of years previous, in 1990, Warrington played Wigan at Wembley and I actually managed to get on from the substitutes' bench. With that goal achieved and Wigan winning that day it was time for a new goal. This time it was to not just play at Wembley, but to actually win. So that was my new ambition. It was great to play at Wembley for the first time, but I had to change my goal because I had found out there is a massive difference between winning and losing there. The stadium was so big and every player aimed to reach the Twin Towers because that is the pinnacle of your rugby playing career as not many players manage to do it. At that point I decided that I would not be satisfied with just one losing appearance at such a magnificent stadium; I needed to taste glory there, so I was determined to return. And fortunately I did.

WE PLAYED the semi-final against Bradford Northern at Burnden Park and won 71-10. That was one of them games when basically everything went right for us. We hardly made any mistakes. Our winger Martin Offiah scored five tries. That said, I really did think it was a fantastic team performance. Every team member pulled for each other and worked really, really hard. The game was won in the first 20 minutes from what I can remember. It was then that it hit me that I was on my way to Wembley again – it was a fantastic feeling.

I hurt my knee the weekend before the Wembley final and I think I only trained on the Wednesday. What the coach at the time, John Monie, used to do in the week building up to Wembley was to have a training session on the

Wednesday and you had to take part in that training session if you wanted to be in contention to play on the Saturday. I had an injection to get rid of some pain and I went and trained. It didn't feel too bad actually. I went into the game with a bit of a sore knee, but I was ok really. The adrenalin got me through, I suppose. As a player you can never tell how many times you will get to play on the hollowed turf of Wembley, so you do whatever you have to do to get through that Wednesday training session knowing you have a couple more days before the game to get yourself right.

We went down to Wembley on the Thursday lunchtime and the send off from the fans was absolutely fantastic. I had never seen anything like it in my life before. Even with Warrington a few years earlier it had not been anything like the send off from Central Park that day. It was amazing; there were thousands of fans lining the car park waving us off as we started our journey by coach down to London. At that time I think the Wigan fans were a special breed of fans. They were so passionate about their rugby, so committed to the team. They just loved rugby league and Wigan in general. I do not think as a player you realise how much the fans really appreciate what you do on the pitch. You become a bit blaze about them, thinking they are just fans. You do not realise how much they buy into it, how much they love it and how much you mean to them. It's only after you finish playing rugby that you think about things like that and think, "my goodness these people have followed us absolutely everywhere and spent a whole lot of money traveling around the world." It's only later you think we should have appreciated the fans more at the time.

The build-up to the game was great. Everyone was alright when it came to our training session down in London and it was really quick and competitive as everyone knew what was at stake. Everyone was relaxed because they had been so many times before. This really helped me because it's a massive occasion. The likes of Dean Bell, Andy Gregory, Andy Platt, Denis Betts and Shaun Edwards helped keep me calm. I thought beforehand that it would be difficult for anyone to beat Wigan at Wembley because of the occasion and how much experience some of these guys had playing at this ground. I was relaxed, which was great and when we went out and won it felt sensational.

It was a great occasion and I remember standing in the tunnel beforehand looking down thinking, "wow, this is fantastic". When I'd played for

Warrington I'd been on the bench, but this time I was in the starting line up and was walking out to start out at number 12. I remember coming out of the tunnel and looking up to the right hand side and seeing the Wigan fans – it was sensational, absolutely sensational.

THE GAME itself, what can I say. We had such a strong team and because of that we were really expected to walk away with an easy victory, but in the end that was not the case. We got off to a great start. Martin Offiah put a kick through to the Castleford line – it was a real harmless one, but Martin never gave up the chase. Their full-back Graham Steadman could not collect the kick and Martin pounced for the first try of the game after only a few minutes. In the opening half we really shocked them and Shaun Edwards sprinted through to get our second try after a neat break from our hooker Martin Dermott. We were leading 12-0 and then Joe Lydon dropped a goal, but minutes later Shaun put a kick deep into Castleford's half and, despite there being a few defenders between him and the ball, Martin Offiah outsprinted them all to grab his second try. I think that effectively won us the game. Frano Botica kicked his third conversion of the half and we went in at the break leading 19-0.

Castleford came out in the second half desperate not to be on the end of a Challenge Cup final drubbing and forced their way over after fine work from Tawera Nikau and Dean Sampson to set up Richie Blackmore to cross. Cas then started to play with a bit more confidence and made a game of it.

Not long after Castleford had scored, Martin Offiah thought he had become the first player in history to score a hat-trick of tries at Wembley. He'd been hotly backed to score a first ever treble after his five try performance in the semi-final. He picked up a loose ball and raced around 50 yards to score, but the try was disallowed after referee Robin Whitfield took advice from his linesman, who ruled it out for a knock-on. But we weren't to be denied. We virtually made the game safe when Steve Hampson, who had come of the substitute's bench, went over in the corner. Castleford refused to lie down and scored their second try of the game through Martin Ketteridge after some fine work from Graham Steadman. Frano Botica added a penalty and Joe Lydon slotted over his second drop-goal to finish the game 28-12 and bring the Challenge Cup back to Wigan.

I can remember during the game I couldn't get my second wind. I was running around the pitch like a headless chicken trying to get my hands on the ball, but it kept missing me all the time. I wasted so much energy running around trying to chase the ball when all I had to do was wait and eventually the ball would come back to me. It was a really warm day at first, but then it rained and became quite stuffy, you know, close, so I remember trying to catch my second wind and I just could not do it.

WEMBLEY IS fantastic! It really is the most amazing place with an incredible atmosphere. I'm not sure if it's just me, but in the past few years when they were rebuilding Wembley and they played the Cup finals at Cardiff and Twickenham I think the Challenge Cup seems to have lost its appeal. There wasn't that many players who got to play at Wembley – it isn't like nowadays in football where they play all the FA Cup semis and also the play-offs at Wembley – they just used to have the FA Cup final, a few England games and the Challenge Cup there, so as a rugby player you only really got one opportunity to play there. It was a hallowed ground and something you always, always wanted to do. There are so many great rugby league players in the past who never got the chance to play at Wembley. I felt very honoured.

We won the game, which was great because it was my new ambition to try and achieve. I remember walking up the steps to receive my medal and kissing the Cup. I also remember Joe Lydon walking down the steps with the Cup at the back of the Wigan team. Joe always went up last, so when he went up it was down to him to bring the Cup down to the rest of team already on the pitch waiting to start the lap of honour.

We had a video camera which we took down with us to do a video diary of the trip. I filmed some stuff after the game capturing the players on the pitch after the final. It was just shots of the team having a laugh and celebrating the win – it was brilliant. At that time our group of players were fantastic. We had a great bunch of individuals that made up an exceptional team. I don't think you'll ever get that kind of closeness again like we had. They were really great people and we had a laugh, which is all part and parcel of winning the Challenge Cup.

WHEN I was at Warrington they offered me a contract which I was not going to sign to be quite honest. It was basically 50% less than what I had been getting the season before. I thought it was ridiculous! I knew Andy Gregory at the time; my dad actually did the plastering at his house. I was working with my dad and one day he phoned me up and said to me that Wigan were interested in signing me. I thought, "oh right" and Andy told me what I had to do to let Wigan know I was interested. I ended up speaking to Maurice Lindsay, came to the club and agreed terms and that was it; I was a Wigan player. I was so pleased to be signing for one of the biggest and best clubs in the world, one with so many international on their books. More than anything, though, I just wanted to be at the club to have the opportunity to win silverware. It was not about the manager or anything like that, it was basically about winning trophies. I wanted to achieve so many things in rugby league and this was hopefully going to be the next step on the ladder to achieving those goals. So it proved.

AFTER THE final, there occured an incident involving the Prime Minister of that time John Major and myself which has gone down in Wigan folklore. The background to the story is that I had a bad cut on my knee. I'd had it for about five weeks beforehand. I had stitches in it, but I didn't want to give up my spot on the team, so I carried on playing with some sponge on my knee to protect it and basically that is all it was – a yellow piece of sponge. It was circular in shape and I made a hole in the middle of it so it would go over my knee. I wore it week after week and we were playing well and reached the Challenge Cup final, so I kept using it. It was something of a lucky charm.

After the game I was having a shower, as you do, and I pulled it off, but thought to myself "I need to keep this because I've been wearing it all the way through our recent good form," so I put it on the end of my manhood, had a wash and walked back into the changing rooms. Just then John Major came in to congratulate us. It was only then I realised the sponge was still on my private parts. I stood there and looked at him and he sort of looked at me and put his hand out for me to shake. I don't know why, but I looked down and he looked down and I said, "it's a pineapple ring, John." As quick as a flash he replied, "well, that's the last time I eat pineapple!" It was an off-the-cuff thing; a little bit of fun. I didn't really think much of it to be honest. At the time I didn't realise there was a TV crew filming at the back of the changing rooms.

Next time I thought about it was when I was on tour Great Britain and I got a phone call. I was rooming with Les Holiday in Papua New Guinea. It was around 5am and I was thinking, "who the hell is this at this time of the morning?" It turned out to be the News of the World wanting to talk about this pineapple ring. I replied, "it's five in the morning and I'm on tour. Leave me alone."

As I put the phone down I started thinking, "how the hell do they know about this?" and tried to get some more sleep. Then the phone rang again and it was another group of papers wanting to talk about the comment. It was then they revealed that the team filming in the changing rooms were actually filming for Up'n'under and it had been shown on television back in England. I wish I had a £1 for every time someone asked me about it. I admit it's not something that happens all the time between the Prime Minister and a sports person! John smiled when he made the comment. Beforehand I'd thought he was a bit boring and a bit grey, but he was great when he said that!

People come up to me all the time and say, "I know about the pineapple ring," so I say, "Oh yes? Tell me." And the usual reply is, "well you had a real pineapple on your ding-a ling" and I'm like, "sod off." Some people still believe it was a real pineapple. The truth is now out!

When I was out on tour my Mum phoned me because there were so many articles about this pineapple ring going round. The Daily Mirror actually did a centre spread, featuring pictures of John Major and myself. One of their journalists had even gone round finding out the diameters of tinned pineapple rings to see which had the biggest hole! I was like "oh my god what is all this about?" It was just a bit of fun, but I'm sure it will go into the history books alongside the names of Billy McGinty and John Major. It was so surreal you could not make it up. I never thought for one minute when I started playing rugby league that I would be meeting the Prime Minister, never mind having double spread newspaper articles with him.

COMING HOME to see the fans was brilliant. The players who had been to Wembley before were used to it, but for me it was really weird. The lads were having a good crack on the way home and there were thousands and thousands of fans coming out to welcome us home and congratulate us. Thinking about it now I am getting goose pimples – it was absolutely sensational. In life there are certain things that will always stay with you and memories like that one that you can't buy. We got back to Central Park and I walked out onto the stage that had been set up there and the pitch was just full of people. I just thought "my goodness".

Those fans were brilliant. I don't think any rugby fans will ever be like those Wigan fans. I think Central Park was a special place for them and it is a shame that Wigan moved from a place like that. It's also a shame the way the team have been playing for the past few years.

A lot of people must think that because Wigan had been to Wembley so many times they were arrogant about the game and felt they had the right to win simply because they were Wigan. That is certainly not true – yes Wigan had the talent, everyone could see that, but we were professional in our approach and respected opponents whoever they might be. As for Wembley, a lot of them who had played there before like Andy Gregory, Shaun Edwards, Andy Platt and Dean Bell were determined not to ever lose at the stadium. Their pride kicked in and they were not going to let anything get in their way.

I LOOK back now at my career with a lot of pride. I was fortunate to have played with some great players in my time at Wigan – not just the squad that won the Challenge Cup in 1992, but also for the other two seasons I was at the club. During my time at Wigan we also became the first club to go to Australia and beat the Aussie champions on their own turf for the World Club Challenge. That was the second time I had won that tournament and it meant the world to me.

I feel very privileged to have been a part of a sensational team and a sensational setup with great coaches and staff. I learned so much off John Monie in our time together at Wigan, not just on the rugby field, but also how to conduct yourself throughout all the aspects of your life. He was a special man to me and still today I think so much of him. It was great to work under him and alongside so many great international players.

I think I need to mention some of the players I played with at Wigan because, as I have said before, we had a great squad. Shaun Edwards was one of the most talented players in the game and when he was on song you knew we had a chance. Also I teamed up with Andy Gregory. I did not get to play with Andy for long because the Challenge Cup win over Castleford was his last in a Wigan shirt, so I only played with him for one season, but you knew what a great player he was and his link up with Edwards was first class.

The pack we had was awesome; we had so much talent that when Great Britain went on tour to Australia in 1992, the second and third Ashes Tests saw the whole pack provided by one club – Wigan. We had Kelvin Skerrett, Martin Dermott and Andy Platt in the front-row, Denis Betts and myself at second-row and Phil Clarke at the back as loose-forward. That was a great feeling for me, but also to have one section of the team made up from one club was unheard of.

The thing is we trained and played hard, but we all had a good sense of humour and that helped us. We had people at Wigan like Martin Dermott, Andy Gregory and Andy Platt – it was like having your own comedians. Everything was a laugh with them and it was a joy to be among their company. A true joy.

BARRIE McDERMOTT
PROP FORWARD 1994–1995

SIGNED From Oldham on 1 July 1994

DEBUT 21 August 1994 versus Featherstone Rovers

WIGAN CAREER 13 appearances, 4 tries

HONOURS Regal Trophy 1994/95, Rugby League Championship
1994/95

LEFT At the end of the 1994/95 season to join Yorkshire rivals Leeds

WHEN PEOPLE first found out about this book I think they would not have expected to be reading a chapter by Barrie McDermott because he only spent one season at Central Park. I chose Barrie to be included because he has always been a larger than life character and I felt he would have some good stories to tell and I was right.

Barrie McDermott must be the only player in history who could hand pick his favourite game in a Wigan shirt as one in which he was put on report and eventually suspended and fined. Barrie was a no nonsense front-row forward and played the game with his heart on his sleeve. Some people may say he was a dirty player, but after reading this chapter you may disagree.

He has been a great servant to the game during his times at Oldham, Wigan, Leeds and Widnes and is still involved in the set-up at the Rhinos. He also does a lot of after-dinner speaking with his old friend Terry O'Connor.

EXPECTATIONS WERE very high ahead of this tour match – it was billed as the unofficial fourth Test before Great Britain took on Australia in the three Ashes Test matches, Many pundits felt Wigan had a very good opportunity to hurt and upset the Aussies before they met Great Britain at Wembley – well someone did get hurt. In a one-sided first half Australia took control, but the one incident which everyone remembers is when Barrie McDermott launched into a tackle which knocked out Australia's enforcer Paul Sironen – just to add extra spice to the series.

Wigan 20 v Australia 30

Ashes Tour Match
Saturday 8 October 1994

Central Park
Attendance 20,057

Teams

Wigan	No.	Australia
Gary Connolly	1	Brett Mullins
Jason Robinson	2	Michael Hancock
Henry Paul	3	Mal Meninga
Va'aiga Tuigamala	4	Steve Renouf
Martin Offiah	5	Wendell Sailor
Frano Botica	6	Laurie Daley
Shaun Edwards	7	Ricky Stuart
Kelvin Skerrett	8	Dean Pay
Martin Hall	9	Steve Walters
Neil Cowie	10	Ian Roberts
Denis Betts	11	Paul Sironen
Andrew Farrell	12	Bradley Clyde
Phil Clarke	13	Brad Fittler
Substitutes		
Steve Hampson	14	Tim Brasher
Barrie McDermott	15	David Fairleigh
Terry O'Connor	16	Steve Menzies
Mick Cassidy	17	David Furner

Wigan		Australia
Connolly, Offiah, Robinson Tuigamala	**Tries**	Clyde, Daley, Hancock Mullins, Pay, Renouf
Botica, Farrell	**Goals**	Meninga 2, Daley

Referee: D Campbell

THE AUSTRALIAN game in 1994 was the first time I had really experienced the incredible atmosphere at Central Park. It opened my eyes.

I'd watched Oldham play Warrington in 1990 in the Challenge Cup semi-final at the ground, but it was little short of empty because there were only Oldham and Warrington fans there. It wasn't a match that was expected to have a massive crowd even though it was a semi-final of a major cup competition and there was no atmosphere to speak of.

On my home debut for Wigan the atmosphere was a bit better at Central Park – this was a few weeks prior to the Wigan versus Australia game. Up until then Central Park did not really reach my expectations, but the game against the Australians was just absolutely electric.

I'd been used to playing at Watersheddings, which was Oldham's home ground. Oldham were the team that I played for and the team from which I signed from and when that ground was full you could see the expressions on people's faces while you were playing. You could see and make out everyone in the crowd because it was right on top of you, but that day at Central Park against Australia the crowd was just a blur – a really colourful, vibrant blur.

AT THE start of the season, having joined Wigan from Oldham, I made one of my targets to get into the Wigan first team to have the chance to play with and against the best players in the world at that time. The 1994 Australian touring side were fantastic; players like David Furner, Mal Meninga, Laurie Daley, Bradley Clyde, Ricky Stuart, Wendell Sailor and Paul Harragon. These were real heroes of mine at the time and players that I really looked up to and respected, so the game was something I definitely wanted to be a part of.

Mal Meninga was becoming the first man to lead an Australian side on two separate tours. They had just been officially nicknamed the Kangaroos, and it was a tradition that they played English club sides to warm up for the test matches against Great Britain. In fact they hadn't lost one of these games since 1978 when they succumbed 11-10 to Widnes and 15-12 to Warrington. They'd warmed up for the British leg of the tour by playing as single Test in France, defeating their hosts by an intimidating 74-0! They weren't a bad side. Before the game against us, they'd also beaten Cumbria 52-8 and Leeds 48-6 in their first two games in England.

My early season form that year was quite good, good enough I believed for me to warrant a place in the side. The night before the game I could not sleep and I had recently passed my driving test, so I chose to go out. I think it was around midnight and I just went out for a bit of a drive to try and relax myself really. Because I was worked up in the early part of my career, I had actually thought long and hard about the game and what it would mean to me and even at this really early stage of my career I kind of played every game as if it was my last. That's my explanation as to why I busted my body so much in those early years, but the apprehension I had for this game was tremendous. All my family were going to be at the game and they were so excited about it. This was also the first time I was going to appear on Grandstand, which for a kid growing up listening to Ray French and all those great commentators was fantastic. I was brought up on that classic video 101 Great Rugby League Tries, so being live on Grandstand was like a dream world really.

It's funny actually how you recall things from the past and how certain things fit into place after the event. The week before we'd played against Sheffield Eagles. I had always been a bit of a shoulder-charger, this was only because I had dislocated my elbow three times early on in my career. It was then that I chose a tackling style that meant I shoulder-charged my opponent who was coming in to meet me. When I was running at full pace into a tackle the thing that I did not do was move my feet, I sort of moved my shoulder and arms into the tackle and ended up catching people quite a lot with the elbow. In the game against Sheffield I caught their prop forward Paul Broadbent.

It was a destructive tackle and it knocked Paul senseless. Our coach at the time, Graeme West, sensibly pulled me to one side and said, "look

Barrie, if that was you and someone had clouted you around your head with their elbow – how would you feel?" I replied, "listen Westy, I didn't mean it. I was running to go and give him a big hit and smash him, but I was not trying to catch him with the elbow."

I absolutely 100% did not mean to it! Westy repeated, "listen I'm not having it – it's not something done by the unwritten rules of the game and it's not fair play," but despite that I retained my place in the team. All the lads who noticed it in the game were mystified at how I got away with it and also how I'd actually done it.

Mick Cassidy was really fascinated, we had a really big punch bag in the gym at Wigan and Mick spent the next week asking me to show him so I did. It's funny really because Mick was then involved in the tackle with Aussie enforcer Paul Sironen during the Australian game which I think was probably the thing that really springboarded my career more than anything. I mean, I like to think I was quite skilful and very aggressive and definitely very passionate, but the thing I probably had on my side above most people of my generation is that fear factor. I think people were not too sure about me even in the latter years when I was trying to be very, very sensible. I think people realised that I did not just talk the talk, I had the bite as well.

The incident itself which everyone still remembers me for was just when I was trying to lift my side that was getting heavily beaten at the time. On the Australian side was Paul Sironen; he was another one of my heroes and five or ten minutes before this actual incident I had been in a bit of a scuffle with him which was just my way really. My heroes and the people I respected tended to be the ones I aimed for and they were the ones I concentrated on. After the scuffle the Aussies scored another try and were leading quite comfortably, We kicked off again for the restart, I think it was either Henry Paul or Frano Botica, and I told him to get plenty of height on the ball because I am going to "F**king smash Paul Sironen." Mick Cassidy came into the tackle with me very low and I sort of had to adjust myself otherwise I would have knocked Mick out cold – I just caught Sironen right with the big thick meat part of the elbow and absolutely pole-axed him. He was out cold.

It was just another one of those situations where nobody could understand, particularly the players on the pitch could not understand, why nobody else had seen what they had just witnessed. Dave Campbell was the referee on that day, he is a great guy and I've seen him many times since, he still swears to this day that he did not see it because it happened so quickly. He could not tell what or who had hit Paul. Funnily enough, when I left Wigan to join Leeds, Campbell was the referee at one game and sent me off for a similar tackle on Paul Sculthorpe. He stated that he hadn't seen that incident either, but he remembered watching the TV replay from the Australia game when he'd got home and thought it must have been me this time as well and sent me off! I think I ended up with a two-match suspension and a £1,000 fine after that incident.

The Australian game itself was my first real taste of the big time – my first taste of playing against people whom I idolised. I didn't know whether to get on with the game of rugby league, try and get their tie-ups or even try and get an autograph or something like that. Mal Meninga was an absolute giant of the game in every sense of the word and to be on the same pitch as him was just a completely different experience to anything I had experienced before.

When I was at Oldham I knew nearly everyone in the crowd or would have known someone who knew them, so to play in front of such a massive crowd at Central Park and to face off against players I really respected was fantastic. After the game I was so high and full of adrenalin even though we had lost heavily – it was billed as the 'fourth Test' and even though we did not live up to the expectations we'd had for ourselves it was such a privilege and something that really springboarded my career.

LOOKING BACK at the game I think at one stage we were getting a real good hiding. It was something like 26-6 to Australia and the omens did not look good for Wigan or Great Britain as they were destroying us with ease. If they could do that to the best club side in the country what would they do in the Test matches? But in the second half we gave a good account of ourselves and our try scorers that day were Gary Connolly, Martin Offiah, Jason Robinson and Va'aiga Tuigamala. I remember Inga's try was a great show of strength and a try that was fit to grace any occasion. We ended up losing the game only 30-20, so to keep the best side in the world to just four points in the second half was a mean feat.

After that game, and due to some of my earlier performances in the season, I was selected to play for Great Britain against Australia in the First

Test at Wembley. I came on as a sub. The Wigan match was still very much in my mind because Ellery Hanley, who was Great Britain coach, told me earlier in the week that I was going to be playing. He said "there is going to be a fair bit of attention for you, Barrie. I trust you to do what I have seen you do at club level and now do it at international level. All you have to do is be yourself." We discussed my feelings about whether I should raise the level of my game to international standard and try to play like an international player or I should just be myself and Ellery insisted that I be myself and let the game flow, "just play your natural game and everything else will fall into place," he said.

Sure enough, when I got on after just 20 minutes, within 20 seconds of taking the field we got a penalty and obviously being a front rower and also being the fresh guy it was up to me to take the ball in. I took the ball and ran it in as hard as I could; the welcoming committee facing me was Paul Harragon, Steve Walters, Glenn Lazarus and Paul Sironen – all were within about 10 metres of each other. I had about three seconds to think to myself, "I'm either going to run and hide from these four guys for the rest of the match or I'm going to take the ball and run at them as hard as I can and let them know that I am no flash in the pan and I'm somebody to be reckoned with". I took the second option and I ran it in like my life depended on it straight at Paul Sironen, who must have been a good two or three stones heavier than me and probably ten inches taller than me as well. As it happened the force and determination that I had in my run actually got me through the other side of Sironen and because I dominated that collision it gave me so much confidence for the rest of the match. It was the first time I had played at Wembley and I came out a winner [Great Britain won 8-4 thanks to a Jonathan Davies try] and it all came from the confidence I had secured in that first confrontation at Central Park.

I WAS only at Wigan for one season – my debut was at Featherstone away and I had a bit of a routine where I would go into the changing rooms, get a programme, go to the toilet, have a sit down and take part in my favourite pastime when I'm on the loo: just reading the programme and digesting what was going on and trying to enjoy the atmosphere. On that day when I looked at the team sheet and saw who was playing I just couldn't believe my name was there, it didn't look in the right place. There were some great, fantastic, awe-inspiring players. When I joined Wigan the first person that I saw after I signed the contract was Shaun Edwards – who I must admit growing up as a lad from Oldham I absolutely detested. At the time everyone looked at Wigan with such jealousy and envy and personally I hated Shaun Edwards because of his character and his flamboyance and also the way he enjoyed his rugby league. He enjoyed hammering the nail into every coffin of every team that he ever played against, including those I supported and played in, but it was also that characteristic that made me respect him so much when I played with him.

When he saw me he shook my hand and welcomed me on board and just said, "look, I hope you'll defend me and your own team-mates as hard as you have tried to attack me on the pitch," and I said "I'll try Shaun," to which he replied "don't call me Shaun – call me Gizmo." That was the character of the lad and of the place really – to the outside world we looked like a team of superstars and collectively or socially we probably did not have much in common, but if you brought something to the party and you were a good player then that earned their respect and made you part of a very tight unit. It was about what you did on the pitch rather than what you were like as a person, where I probably think it was the opposite when I was at Oldham, people wanted to know you as a person and look after you, take on board the character or what you were about, rather than what you did out on the pitch. Perhaps that is why Wigan were so successful for so long.

As far as summing up my career as a rugby league player myself, Terry O'Connor talked a lot about it five years ago. It must have been in the middle of one of my suspensions when he turned around and said to me, "do you not worry that you are going to be remembered as a dirty player and not a skilful, good, hard one?" I said, "the thing is Tez, I need that prominence and I need to 100% show my teeth and do that in every match I play, but inevitably when you show your teeth and growl at people you are going to have to bite someone once every so often"

I think I accepted for a fact that once or twice every season I would have to spend some time out suspended. Kelvin Skerrett, who was a great front rower at Wigan advised me that as a front rower if you aren't getting sent off a least once a season then you are not fulfilling that reputation, you are not showing people you are what you say you are.

As far as being remembered as a dirty player, I don't place too much importance on being dirty or skilful or anything like that. I just know that every time I played for whichever team I played for I would always give 100%, I was determined in everything I did, whether it was getting the better of an opposing player or to come off the pitch a winner with my team-mates. No-one can ever accuse me of not giving my all and at the end of the day I have had an absolute ball playing rugby league. I am very passionate about the sport and I regret nothing. I learnt some pretty harsh lessons along the way, but I think ultimately the person that I am justifies the means.

EVERYONE in rugby league knows about my friendship with Terry O'Connor, probably because we are always on the television together. Me and Tez first met when we were about 15 or 16 years-old and he was the most annoying man in the world! That's the first thing that came across to me, but eventually I came to appreciate his sense of humour; either that or he has made more of an effort to make me laugh than anybody because we just enjoy each other's company so much. Now that we are fathers and husbands we are probably embroiled in each others lives more than anything, but the thing that cemented our friendship at Wigan was that it seemed to be either O'Connor or McDermott in the starting line-up, but this never affected our growing friendship and testament to it was that we never resented the one for getting in ahead of the other.

I can go back to the Regal Trophy final victory over Warrington. I had been out for a period of time with an injury and Tez had been playing really well so he was selected for the final. But unfortunately he pulled his hamstring the week before and Graeme West said to him, "look, if you're not fit I do not want you to play. I have got Barrie who is fit and raring to go, so it's a straight choice between you and him. If you tell me you are not fit then he's in." Tez discussed it with me and said, "I'm going to give myself until the last minute because I want to play, but if I'm not right rather than take the money and risk getting injured and get carried off after a few minutes I would rather you play".

I played in that game in the end and really enjoyed it. I scored a try and got my medal. That is just one story of our friendship. The thing I can say about Tez is that he is very similar to me. We are the types that negative issues make us more determined to succeed the next time we get the chance and he did that. He eventually played in a Regal Trophy Final and even got the Man of the Match award and I was absolutely thrilled to bits for him.

We are really close and have such a great friendship. We never want to give bragging rights to the other one and that's how we do it. I think if both of us were going to war tomorrow we would want to take each other with us, maybe only to push the other one over the fence first, but it's a friendship that will probably last for as long as we are both alive. It is definitely cemented by our love of rugby league, what it has given us and the lessons we have learned about each other. We have always done everything side by side.

I think that is enough good talk about Terry, I feel it should be my duty to slag him off a bit now. I can say it was a real pleasure to play with Tez at Widnes during my swansong when I came out of retirement to team up with him again – or basically to carry him through the games. It was interesting to know that he had gained a new nickname – at Widnes he was known as Skip; it wasn't because he was captain of the team and led from the front, it was because he was full of s**t.

SHAUN EDWARDS

STAND-OFF/SCRUM HALF 1983–1997

SIGNED At midnight on his 17th birthday in October 1983 for a reported £35,000 from Wigan St. Patrick's ARL

DEBUT 6 November 1983 versus York

WIGAN CAREER 467 appearances, 274 tries, 27 goals (includes 4 drop goals)

HONOURS World Club Challenge 1987, 1991, 1994 Rugby League Championship 1986/87, 1989/90, 1990/91, 1991/92, 1992/93, 1993/94, 1994/95, 1995/96 Challenge Cup 1985, 1988, 1989, 1990, 1991, 1992, 1993, 1994, 1995 Premiership Trophy 1987, 1992, 1994, 1995, 1996 John Player/Regal Trophy 1985/86, 1986/87, 1989/90, 1992/93, 1994/95, 1995/96 Lancashire Cup 1985, 1986, 1987, 1988, 1992 Charity Shield 1985, 1987, 1991

LEFT Joined London Broncos in March 1997 for £60,000

SHAUN EDWARDS will go down in history as one of the most talented and most loved Wigan players of all-time. 'Giz', as he was known, signed for his home-town club from amateur side Wigan St. Patrick's on his 17th birthday in October 1983. The £35,000 fee Wigan reportedly paid was believed to the highest ever for an amateur player.

Shaun continued to impress after breaking into the first-team and made Challenge Cup final appearances at Wembley in 1984 and 1985 being a loser and a winner before leading the club out at the same venue in 1988 against Halifax to become the youngest ever captain to lift the Challenge Cup at the Twin Towers in a win which began Wigan's famous eight victories in a row

For such a talented player Shaun never actually won the Lance Todd Trophy award, but special praise must go to him after playing the majority of the 1990 final with a fractured cheekbone and eye socket. Despite those twin problems, he had a fantastic game. He holds a joint club record for the most tries in a match – he scored 10 tries against Swinton, equalling Martin Offiah's 10 scored against Leeds in a Premiership game.

Shaun collected the Man Of Steel award in 1990 and even received an OBE in January 1996 for his services to rugby league. He left the club in 1997 to join London Broncos before agreeing a deal to join Bradford Bulls and then finished his playing career back with the Broncos. He featured in the last Challenge Cup final at the old Wembley in 1999 before it was demolished.

Shaun became a successful coach in rugby union with London Wasps, winning the 2007 Heineken European Cup and in late 2006 ruled himself out of the vacant Great Britain rugby league job. A lot of Wigan supporters still hold a glimmer of hope that if he does return to the 13-a-side code it will be with his home-town club.

WIGAN HAD won the first ever World Club Challenge match in 1987 against Manly at Central Park, before adding their second triumph in 1991 against Penrith. In between Widnes won a Challenge match in 1989. Brisbane did get a little bit of revenge for the Aussies when they defeated Wigan in 1992, but every time a British club won the title the Australians would use the excuse that they had not adapted well to the conditions in England after a hard season down under.

Well, in 1994 Wigan were invited to go to Australia and attempt to win it the hard way – after their own hard season which had seen them win a record-breaking seventh successive (of the eventual eight) Challenge Cup finals and a fifth successive rugby league Championship. Could they beat the Broncos in their own backyard or had all the Australians excuses been legitimate reasons after all?

Wigan 20 v Brisbane Broncos 14

World Club Challenge
Wednesday 1 June 1994

ANZ Stadium
Attendance 54,220

Teams

Gary Connolly	1	Willie Carne
Jason Robinson	2	Wendell Sailor
Sam Panapa	3	Steve Renouf
Barrie-Jon Mather	4	Chris Johns
Martin Offiah	5	Michael Hancock
Frano Botica	6	Kevin Walters
Shaun Edwards	7	Allan Langer
Neil Cowie	8	Glenn Lazarus
Martin Dermott	9	Kerrod Walters
Billy McGinty	10	Andrew Gee
Denis Betts	11	Mark Hohn
Andy Farrell	12	Alan Cann
Phil Clarke	13	Julian O'Neill
	Substitutes	
Martin Hall	14	John Plath
Mick Cassidy	15	Peter Ryan
Paul Atcheson	16	Brett Galea
Va'aiga Tuigamala	17	Chris McKenna
Betts, Mather, Robinson	**Tries**	Sailor, Hancock, O'Neill
Botica 4	**Goals**	O'Neill

Referee: G McCallum

ONE OF the games I have fondest memories of during my time playing for Wigan is the Brisbane Broncos clash for the World Club Championship over in Australia in 1994. Thinking about that game always makes me smile and helps me recall the fond memories I have of that period when we were pretty much the best team in the world.

The World Club Championship was between the champions of the Australian season, which was the Broncos, and the English champions, which was us. We had just finished a really tough season, John Dorahy had been in charge for most of the campaign, but Graeme West had then taken over and we went back to all our old ways of training and because of that we had won the championship and the Challenge Cup. We'd played over 40-odd games and it was the end of a real gruelling season.

When we arrived in Australia, beforehand we had planned to do all this travelling around and have certain training sessions, but then Greame took over the reigns and he binned all that and suggested what we really needed was a little bit of rest and relaxation, so we went to a great resort on the Gold Coast. We trained as soon as we got there and then as a reward he decided to give us two days off – this was meant as a time for the players to bond and we certainly did that! It was a very good team exercise. We all relaxed quite a bit and had a few drinks and basically enjoyed ourselves. We knew we had been handed a position of trust and we did not break that trust, we just made sure we all had a good time within the boundaries.

On the Sunday before the game, which was to be played on a Wednesday, suddenly that was it. Graeme had slapped a total alcohol ban on the whole squad and from that moment on we were all focused on the task in hand. We trained on that Sunday night and credit to the boys we prepared exceptionally well for the game as we knew we were in for a hell of a test. We were heading into this game as heavy underdogs to be honest and that had not really happened to Wigan during the season. We were always the ones up there to be shot down. One of the main reasons we were such big underdogs was that all our front-row forwards were missing – Andy Platt and Kelvin Skerrett were both out injured and also Dean Bell was deemed not fit to play – so really we had a numerous amount of players missing through injuries and what have you.

As I said, Brisbane were massive favourites to reclaim the title they won against us at Central Park in 1992. I must admit we were very nervous and anxious heading into the game. We knew that if we did not perform to the level we were capable of not only could we lose the game, but we could end up getting really battered, for want of a better word. So we had that fear factor behind us and what I also knew was that if we played anywhere near our full potential as regards keeping our error rate low and building pressure on their defence, we had a great chance of winning the World Club Challenge again because at the back end of the English season we had put in some really strong performances and no matter where you are in the world if you can control the ball well and exert pressure from your defence you can win, whether it be the ANZ Stadium, Central Park or even Knowsley Road. The vital thing in our minds was not to give the Australians any easy ball by continually dropping it or losing it on contact because if you do that, particularly against a team like the Brisbane Broncos with the players they had, they would most definitely punish us.

EVENTUALLY IT got to kick-off time and we were all pumped up and ready to show the Australians what we were made of on their own soil. We got off to a dream start, I think within the first 16 minutes we were 12-0 up, which certainly shocked the Broncos. Our second-row forward Denis Betts opened the scoring with a well-collected try after he chased one of my kicks. He snuck up behind the Broncos' defence to touch down and our goal machine Frano Botica added the extras. Minutes later we had scored again when Barrie-Jon Mather glided through a gap after a neat break from Phil Clarke. We were in dream land after Frano made it 12-0. I think the important thing about the opening 20 minutes was that we were not geniuses with the ball, we just kept it simple. Whereas they kept dropping the ball and handing possession back to us, so then any chances that came our way we finished them off clinically.

Wendell Sailor crossed over from close range to give Brisbane a bit of hope before the half-time break, but just two minutes into the second period our winger Jason Robinson, who quite remarkably was left out of the Wigan first-team before Westy took control, scored one of those tries that only Jason could score. Brisbane and Australia winger Michael Hancock dropped the ball and Jason scooped up possession to race clear unopposed. The only player to get a hand on him was our hooker Martin Hall who pounced on him after he scored the try. After that we just defended manfully. They were frantically attacking our line on numerous occasions, but we just kept killing them. They did manage to fight back with late scores from Michael Hancock and Julian O'Neill, but a penalty from Frano Botica sealed a 20-14 win. It was kind of sweet revenge after the Broncos had come over to England in 1992 and beaten us on our own patch at Central Park for the same title – we had now become the first and only British team to go to Australia and reign victorious.

AFTER THE game there was obviously great elation, particularly with the fact that we had triumphed in Brisbane in front of a packed house. The boys were out celebrating that fact specifically because we all thought we were going to get a really big winning bonus because the amount was decided on how big the crowd was. The ground was jam-packed full with just under 60 thousand people – there was never any doubt it was full – so after the game all the boys went on a bit of a spending spree. Between the squad we spent a lot more money than we could probably afford, expecting to get this huge winning cheque when we returned to Wigan. Unfortunately when we did get back, I don't know what happened on the Broncos side of things, but we ended up getting far, far less than we had actually anticipated and in the end it probably cost every one of us money to go out there! But it was worth it because it was a memory that will stick with you for the rest of our lives really.

It is amazing looking back at the experience to be honest. I remember Billy McGinty played in the front-row for what was probably the first time in his career as he was usually a very good second-row forward. Billy had not played much for the first team that season, but during that World Club Challenge match he gave a whole-hearted display and it was typical of the spirit we had in that team. I also thought Neil Cowie was outstanding alongside him during the game. Another player who stood up to be counted at the ANZ Stadium was Barrie-Jon Mather. He'd had a fantastic season for us that year, scoring some vital tries along the way. It was fortunate for us that he took that form into the Brisbane game and scored that spectacular try which gave us such a wonderful start.

Looking at that Brisbane side they had some fantastic stars on show. They were packed full of internationals including Willie Carne, Michael Hancock, Allan Langer, Kevin and Kerrod Walters, Glenn Lazarus and two players who eventually went over to England to play for Wigan; Steve Renouf and Julian O'Neill. But one player who impressed me that day was a young Wendell Sailor. He was only 19 at the time. The press had built him up so much about what he was going to do to Martin Offiah, but to be fair it did not affect Wendell and he had a really impressive game. He was just awesome and caused a huge number of problems, which showed when he scored in the first-half. I think his performance for the Broncos that day showed the whole world what a great player he was about to become.

Leading up to the game the Australian media had written us off at every given opportunity and as captain of the side I was handed the task of handling most of the interviews. I basically tried to lull them into a false sense of security. When the Australians come over to England for the World Club Challenge they always have their excuses written out, so I thought I would turn it around on them for a change. I said, "oh well, it is the end of our season and it has been really tough. We are just here for a good time," and all that kind of thing, but deep down I knew we were all ready and focused on performing well and beating Brisbane. We all think it is rubbish when they come over with their excuses about not having enough time to acclimatise – you can fly over to Australia and play three days later and win, it is not too bad. We proved it!

I HAVE got a great relationship with the World Club Challenge. I played in four and won three of them. The first one was in 1987 against Manly when we won 8-2 in front of 36,895 at Central Park. The second win was at Liverpool football club's Anfield ground when we defeated Penrith. My third game was when we lost to Brisbane at Central Park, then my final one was this one in Australia, so I have done quite well. I think these World Club Challenge victories proved Wigan were better than any club side in the world at that time. Being honest, looking back, the best Wigan sides I ever played in did not actually win a World Club Challenge. Our 1988 team was a very strong unit and also in 1995 we were a major force to be reckoned with, but in those years there was not a tournament held, so I believe if there had been an annual World Club Challenge match Wigan would probably have more than the three we have now.

Going over and winning the title in Australia certainly proved a point in my eyes because they were constantly moaning saying how the game is always held in England, how British clubs have the advantage and that is why Aussies never win it. Well, we went over there and beat the best they had to offer after completing 44 games in England.

The defeat Wigan had suffered in 1992 was always in the back of my mind. I actually got to know some of the Brisbane players when I first joined the London Broncos and they said that game at Central Park was one of the toughest games they had ever played in and a lot of Australians believe the NRL is a far stronger competition than our Super League. In many ways the game in Brisbane was a role-reversal of the game in Wigan. In Brisbane we took our chances and they didn't, but it was the other way round in 1992. We put pressure on them early doors, but kept dropping the ball at crucial times and that is the difference in the big games – whoever plays simple rugby and does the basics correctly will win. Brisbane did it in Wigan, Wigan did it in Brisbane.

PREPARATION WAS very important because I knew I had to be totally focused, I knew a lot of the players were going into unknown territory. I tried to use my experience of having played in so many massive games to give them all a bit of confidence. I suppose that's what captains are there for. A lot of the guys were really apprehensive about playing a team with the calibre of the Brisbane Broncos at the ANZ Stadium – where I have been fortunate to have been on a tour and win games too. It was really important that I stressed to the rest of the guys that if we repeat the stuff we do in England – accuracy, completing sets of six, chasing kicks well and being strong in defence – that it actually works in Australia just as it does in England. Some of them were nervous at the start, but I eventually got through to them and it was a strong performance in the end. It has to be one of the most memorable games I have ever played in.

I did feel quite a bit of pressure going into the game, but with that kind of pressure you either buckle under it or it makes you stronger and I always felt I handled the pressure quite well during my career when my back was against the wall. The atmosphere in the ANZ Stadium was quite subdued really because it was our job to try and shut the crowd up and we effectively did that by getting off to a flying start with those quick tries. I must admit we were hanging on at the end, but it was a fantastic feeling to win over there.

The response was fantastic, most people say they watched it on TV and they always mention we got the main sports slot on the news and things like that, which was special because rugby league hardly ever got headline news. I think everyone was shocked really, but we showed what a bunch of competitive lads we had in that team. Even after the game the Australians were still moaning. They actually came out with the excuse that most of the Brisbane players had just played in a State of Origin series between New South Wales and Queensland. Even after our great performance they still would not give us any credit! I said, "we have just have played 44 games and travelled 12,000 miles." They are on a different level. It is unbelievable. They are not the best at sportsmanship.

I STILL watch the World Club Championship matches nowadays and I actually thought the Wests Tigers side that came over to face Bradford in 2006 was one of the worst ever NRL champions to come over, but full credit to Bradford they stuck to their game plan and won the title. I always want the British side to win because it is always good to get one over on the Aussies – even when St Helens faced Brisbane this year I still wanted Saints to win despite being a die-hard Wigan lad.

Hopefully it will not be too long before Wigan are competing in another World Club Championship game to add to our three previous wins. I think in Brian Noble they have a great coach and we will start being a force again. And if the fans continue to follow them that could happen soon. The supporters were fantastic in 2006 and played their part in helping Wigan avoid relegation from Super League after that poor start and they certainly deserve some success for their loyalty over the years.

TERRY O'CONNOR

FORWARD 1994–2004

SIGNED In August 1994 from Salford for a reported fee of £74,000
DEBUT September 4 1994 v Oldham
WIGAN CAREER 306 appearances, 13 tries
HONOURS Super League 1998 Rugby league championship 1994/94,
1995/96 Challenge Cup 2002 Premiership 1996, 1997 Regal Trophy
1995/96 Charity Shield 1995 Great Britain tourist 1996 Ireland captain
World Cup 2000 Lancashire representative honours
LEFT Joined hometown club Widnes in 2005

TERRY O'CONNOR arrived at Central Park in 1994 as a relative unknown, but by the time he left to join his hometown club Widnes in 2005 he was recognised as one of the best props in Super League and a clear fans favourite on the terraces at Wigan.

O'Connor was adored by the supporters because of his hard work and determination once he donned the famous Cherry and White shirt. He always gave 100%. He led from the front and was rightly rewarded with a testimonial year at the end of his Warriors career. Not only was O'Connor known for his hard running and tough tackling, he was also renowned around the club as a bit of a joker – as a number of team-mates and supporters found out when he was handed a microphone during his many dinners during his testimonial year.

WIGAN HAD finished top of the league, but from this season a new and innovative play-off format was introduced, so Wigan clashed with second-placed Leeds for a place in the Premiership Grand Final at Old Trafford, while the loser had a second chance the following week.

Wigan Warriors 17 v Leeds Rhinos 4

Super League Qualifying Semi-final
Friday 11 October 1998

Central Park
Attendance 12,941

Teams

Kris Radlinski	1	Iestyn Harris
Jason Robinson	2	Paul Sterling
Danny Moore	3	Richie Blackmore
Gary Connolly	4	Brad Godden
Mark Bell	5	Francis Cummins
Henry Paul	6	Daryl Powell
Tony Smith	7	Ryan Sheridan
Terry O'Connor	8	Martin Masella
Robbie McCormack	9	Terry Newton
Tony Mestrov	10	Darren Fleary
Lee Gilmour	11	Adrian Morley
Stephen Holgate	12	Anthony Farrell
Andy Farrell	13	Marc Glanville
	Substitutes	
Paul Johnson	14	Andy Hay
Simon Haughton	15	Marcus St Hilaire
Neil Cowie	16	Leroy Rivett
Jon Clarke	17	Jamie Mathiou
Gilmour, Bell, Paul	**Tries**	Cummins
Farrell 2	**Goals**	
Farrell	**Drop Goal**	

Referee: S Cummings

AFTER THINKING about it for a while I decided my most memorable game was when we played Leeds at Central Park in the play-off semi-final in 1998.

It was the year John Monie returned as coach of the club and everyone expected him to come over and be the hero, bringing the great days back when he took over from Eric Hughes. People still thought he had the glory of what he had when he built the Wigan side in the previous years during the nineties.

The first cup final we played in that season was the Challenge Cup final against Sheffield Eagles and we got beat. It's a result that still haunts me to this day. This was Wigan's first Challenge Cup final since they'd masterminded that remarkable run of eight consecutive cup final victories, so to lose to the massive underdogs form Sheffield was a major shock.

After the final defeat everyone was disappointed. I didn't actually play much in the final. I never really got on with John Monie – it was a clash of personality. I think I made a joke about his size when he first arrived at the club and I don't think he ever forgive me for it, coupled with the fact I did not really have a good Australian talking voice. That didn't help. I just didn't spend much time with him.

I was really fed up and I actually nearly signed for Bradford that season. After the defeat to Sheffield I spent about five weeks playing for the Wigan Under 21s. John had only used me for 12 minutes in the cup final at Wembley and I had a bit of a whinge because I am just like any other player, I want to play in the big games and they don't get much bigger than the Challenge Cup Final at Wembley. He then dropped me. It was like he took everything out on me by putting me in the 21s, which was against Sheffield away. It was in the middle of nowhere and the only people there were my mum and dad watching and the fourth official.

After that I was virtually in my car on the way to sign to Bradford, I was told I could leave Wigan by John Monie, so I thought at that time I had totally had enough of not playing for the first team and felt I was rotting in the 21s. No disrespect to the 21s, but I didn't need it at that time. I'd played for Great Britain and felt I deserved more than that. But, like I say, the thing that set us apart was when I made a joke about him being small. I remember Neil Cowie coming up to me and saying, "Mate, you don't talk to Mr Monie like that,' and looking back I think he was dead right.

So I nearly went to Bradford and I also nearly signed for St Helens and this was all because of what was happening. It wasn't a case of me throwing my toys out of the pram, I just wanted to play. Andy Goodway who was the assistant coach to John Monie at the time, was a great help. He would be honest with you and say if you was playing rubbish. He would tell you why you weren't playing or why you were on the bench. He was brilliant because you knew were you stood. Monie wasn't like that, but to be fair I wouldn't go and ask him why I wasn't playing; I just spoke to Andy Goodway. I wasn't being rude to John Monie, but I would just get the right answers from Andy Goodway.

I was literally going to my car to meet my agent at Birch Services to sign a contract at Odsal with Bradford, but I got a phone call from the club saying I couldn't go and had to go back to Wigan for training. They wouldn't sell me; even though there was a fee agreed and everything. They also wouldn't let me sign for St Helens. I was fed up and I would have gone anywhere just to leave the club, but looking back, after all the time I spent at Wigan, I could never have played for St Helens, even now my daughter supports Saints and it does my head in. Everyone in our village supports St Helens, so she now she loves them. I just cannot get my head around it.

So the club wouldn't sell me. It was strange because I couldn't get in the first team, but they were not willing to let me leave; it was so frustrating. I had another chat with Andy Goodway, who told me to just knuckle down and I would get a chance. I did that and I started to play some good rugby, which culminated in playing for Great Britain against the Kiwis at the end of the year. It was the confidence Goodway gave me that made me come back stronger, because before that I didn't have the confidence because I wasn't enjoying it.

Andy was right. I eventually got my chance and took it with both hands, so when the Leeds game came around I was really psyched up for it because they had already beaten us twice that season. The first was a 16-8 defeat at Headingley in round six of Super League, with Simon Haughton grabbing our only try. We also had Andy Farrell sent to the sin-bin which didn't help our cause. They then came to Central Park and defeated us 15-8, Simon Haughton once again scoring our only try. I suppose looking back I wanted to have a big game because I wasn't in the squad for the Headingley clash, and I started from the bench at Central Park. There was a bit of history for this semi-final because Robbie McCormack had been knocked out in our last game against them. We knew they had a big pack with the likes of Martin Masella, Adrian Morley and Jamie Mathiou. Everyone knows that me and Barrie McDermott are very good friends, but being honest I love playing against Baz because I know he brings the best out of me and we always give 100% to bash the other, but on this day McDermott didn't play which was good from a team's point of view.

There was a bit of needle between the teams also because of an incident between Mick Cassidy and Adrian Morley in the previous game between us – Cass never meant to hit Moz with an elbow, he's not that kind of player. He went to jump up and turned his back because he was petrified, and as he turned he caught Adrian with his elbow. It was Moz's fault; he should never lead with his chin! There was a clip on the end of season video when it panned to Moz and he was sat on his backside with his legs crossed and his hands between his legs like a school kid and he was laughing. I was sat on the bench and started laughing with him. I couldn't believe this guy had just been knocked out and he's sat there laughing! So it started me off and we both couldn't stop. Cass didn't get sent off, but he was cited and got suspended for six games, but he managed to return for the final.

Another thing during that year which I was unhappy about was when John Monie took the number eight jersey off me and gave it to Tony Mestrov – since Super League started in 1996 we had all been given squad numbers. That really upset me because I had worn the number eight shirt for the past two years and I never wanted to lose it, he gave me the number 16 jersey instead. Everyone would be upset whether it is in rugby or not, if you got a demotion at work you would feel filthy and that's what I felt like. It felt like I was being demoted. So that was another point I thought I needed to prove – that I was worth of wearing the number eight shirt for Wigan.

I HAVE always been quite lucky that I have lived in the same town all my life and I feel very fortunate to have played rugby, so I wanted everything in my career to go smoothly and most of the time it has. But that bad year helped me focus by taking the knock of getting demoted knowing that by the time we got to the semi-final I was back in the side again and that I was not going to lose my place.

That Leeds play-off game was incredible. Like most games it was a bit of a blur, because you are so involved with the moment and what you are trying to do, so I can't actually remember much of it – except that is for the major incidents.

After about 15 or 20 minutes I picked Daryl Powell out of their line and ran straight at him and he knocked me out. It was the best tackle in the whole world I've ever seen – it knocked me clean out and I went down like a tree had been felled. I got up wobbly and our hooker Robbie McCormack had to hold me up. All I could see was Jamie Mathiou stood in front of me. I said to him, "I'm going to knock you out if carry on you Aussie so-and-so," and Powell burst out laughing. Mathiou looked straight at me and said, "it wasn't even f***ing me."

So I went off and as I was sat on the bench I started feeling weird and thinking different things like, "why am I here?" I was looking around thinking, "why are we playing Leeds now?" It was a case of "what are they doing in my bedroom?" I eventually went back on and another incident I remember was when Terry Newton, who is now a good mate of mine and was playing for Leeds at the time, stamped on my hand after a tackle. It happened after I ran straight over the top of him with the ball as he tackled me and he came round the back of me as I was lying on the floor. I put my hand down to play the ball as I got up and he stamped on it and ran off. I've shown it him quite a few times on the video and he still claims it was accidental!

THE ATMOSPHERE at Central Park was phenomenal. We had started to hit a bit of form going into that game and they were always close matches when Wigan and Leeds met each other. The thing at Central Park was you always knew when you were in for a big crowd because when you come out of the tunnel and looked up into the top left hand corner if there were people stood there you knew it was chocker full in the ground. When the place was full, walking out it into the stadium was absolutely brilliant.

THINKING ABOUT the lead up to that game against Leeds, personally what went through my mind was the fact that it was the first ever semi-final for the new Grand Final, because that year was the first time they introduced the new format. No-one had ever played in a Grand Final and I wanted to grasp this opportunity. And, because I hadn't played much of a role in the Challenge Cup Final, I'd been devastated. But I was now playing well and I knew there was a big event at the end of the year. I was back in the team and, after all the disappointment I'd suffered that season, I could nearly reach out and grab success.

The team felt that night that we were unstoppable; it was a fantastic night. We were the underdogs and there were so many thoughts running through my mind. I just remember being so determined to be playing in that first ever Grand Final at Old Trafford a few weeks later.

I can vaguely remember Lee Gilmour scoring a fantastic long-range try, going round Anthony Farrell. That was the night Lee Gilmour came of age; he was absolutely phenomenal. He was always strong as an ox, Gilly, he were great. The same goes for Robbie McCormack; he was tough as nails and was a fantastic player. He'd played against us for Hunter Mariners in the World Club Challenge the year before and we knew then he was something special.

The victory was so fantastic. We had not beaten them all season and they really thought they had the edge on us. They didn't necessarily believe they just had to turn up, they knew it would be a tough game, but they had done all the little things right all season to be one step ahead of us.

We just stunned them that night with our physical presence and how passionate and, yes, good we were. It was one of the most emotional games I have ever been involved in.

I think Leeds were the best team overall that year. We had lost the previous two times we'd played them that season, but we managed to see them off that night. I've been lucky enough to play in Grand Finals since then, but to then go and on and play in the first ever final was fantastic.

IT IS honestly the best game I have ever played in and I say that having obviously played for Great Britain. But for Wigan it is by far and away the most enjoyable one I've played in because no-one gave us a chance after we had lost to Sheffield Eagles in the Challenge Cup final. I felt I proved a point to certain people and myself personally. After the game I was up in the bar; I hadn't really been focusing on getting in the Great Britain squad because I was more interested in my form for Wigan, but I was told to get ready for a meeting on Monday because I'd been selected for the Great Britain squad, so I knew I must have done something right because there were a lot of good props around in 1998.

It was quite special because I always remember Kelvin Skerrett saying to me, "it's only ever one man's opinion of you – if you get dropped for a big game or you don't get picked for Great Britain or something goes wrong in your career don't worry do not ever doubt yourself." He was great with me, Kelvin, for things like that. I thought, "yeah, he's right. It is only one man's opinion of me." I knew I had played for Great Britain before and felt I had a point to prove and I wanted that first ever Grand Final.

I always remember those words Kelvin said. You have to imagine going to work and having a really bad week. You wouldn't be in the best mood would you? And I felt I was stuck in a rut. I wasn't playing well and I knew the reasons why I wasn't playing well because I wasn't enjoying it and the harder and harder I tried the more frustrated I was becoming.

John Monie wrote about me in his book that he always knew that: "[O'Connor] didn't know where I stood with him, but he came of age that night in the semi-final when he took on the Leeds pack on his own." He never said that to my face, but it was good of him to put it in his book. But for me, players need to hear those words of confidence. Everyone is entitled to their own opinion, though.

I HAD some great times at Wigan. When I was asked to pick one game I wanted it to be special, it's easy to pick a Grand Final or cup win, but that Leeds game was my favourite for all those reasons. There is another moment that sticks in my memory and it was the Regal Trophy final in 1995 – it was my first major final. After the game Joe Lydon came up to me and handed me the match ball and told me to keep it. At first I thought, "what you giving me that for?" But Joe said, "Don't worry, you will look back on this in a few years time and think 'what a great bloke that old fellow was!'" It's the best thing in the world that first ball. I've kept it to this day in a trophy cabinet to remind me of my first big game.

But I had to choose the Leeds game because of what it meant with us being massive underdogs and me almost signing for Saints and Bradford, plus being dropped to the 21s. If I had jumped in my car and headed over to Bradford and signed a deal that would have been it; this game would never have been mentioned. I was just an hour's travelling time from leaving Wigan, so it's unbelievable. Also, looking back on that year, I almost signed for Warrington. I met the Wolves coach Darryl Van de Velde in the Daresbury Hotel all because of my relationship with John Monie about two weeks before the Bradford deal came on the table. Clubs had started to realise that I was only playing in the Under 21s and knew that I must have been a decent player if the likes of Bradford, Saints and Warrington were coming in for me. I was never told why Wigan stopped me leaving, plus I never questioned it. It's weird how things change because at the end of that season they got rid of Stephen Holgate and gave me a three-year deal, despite the fact I still had another year to go. So in the last seven or eight games I had gone from nearly being sold to earning a new three year deal. It's bonkers.

There was a moment which summed everything up that season. I remember after the Wembley defeat to Sheffield my missus was upstairs at home crying. She was gutted that I didn't get more of a run out that day. I thought from that moment I was never going to let that happen to me again in a final; I was not having my missus upset like that because I had only played 12 minutes in a Challenge Cup Final at Wembley. I was not having my family upset like that over a game of rugby, so I thought, "I'm going to show you," and I have never been dropped like that for a final ever since.

DAVID FURNER

SECOND ROW FORWARD 2001–2002

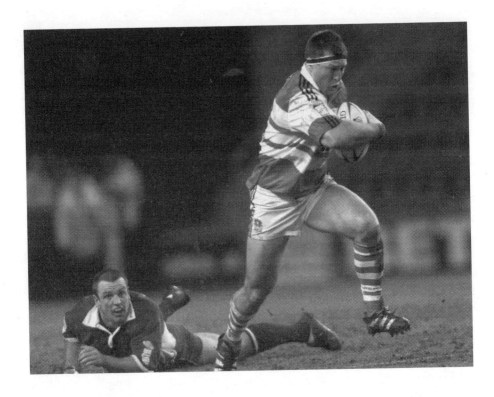

SIGNED From Canberra Raiders ahead of the 2001 Super League
      season
DEBUT 10 February 2001 versus St Helens
WIGAN CAREER 58 appearances, 21 tries, 13 goal
HONOURS Challenge Cup 2002, Australia caps
LEFT Joined Leeds at the end of the 2002 season

DAVID FURNER was a coach's delight; a hard-working, fast running, big-hitting forward who would put his body on the line for his team-mates. He also weighed in with quite a few tries and was very handy with a kicking tee.

Furner arrived in England from Aussie giants Canberra Raiders with a very big reputation. He had represented both Australia and New South Wales and goes down in history as the highest-scoring forward in the history of Australian Rugby League with an incredible 1,219 points in 200 appearances for the Raiders, including 49 tries, 511 goals and one drop-goal. He was also awarded the Clive Churchill medal for his Man-of-the-Match performance in the 36-12 Australian Grand Final victory in 1994 over Canterbury Bulldogs at the Sydney Football Stadium.

During his stay at the JJB Stadium, Furner appeared on the losing side in the 2001 Super League Grand Final, losing to Bradford Bulls at Old Trafford. Current Wigan centre/full-back Michael Withers scored a hat-trick for the Bulls that day, though Furner did eventually taste the success of silverware with a 21-12 victory over St Helens at the home of Scotland Rugby Union in the Challenge Cup ending a run of four years without a trophy, and at the time of writing, the 2002 victory at Murrayfield was the last trophy Wigan have won.

WIGAN VERSUS St Helens in a Challenge Cup final is always a special occasion, it does not matter if you are from Ashton, Scholes, Haydock, Parr, Queensland or New South Wales, you still know what this game means in terms of rivalry and David Furner is no exception.

In this chapter 'Disco' David Furner, as he was fondly named by the Wigan faithful, recalls the day his father, former Australia coach Don, arrived back home from a tour to England with a replica Wigan shirt. Little did he know that years later he would be wearing the same jersey as he ran out in front of thousands of Wiganers screaming his name at Murrayfield for the final of Britain's greatest competition.

Furner looks back at his brief spell at the club and remembers winning his first and only trophy with the club. He looks back with admiration at the character of full-back Kris Radlinski, who got out of his hospital bed to put in a courageous Man-of-the-Match performance to bring the trophy back home to the correct side of Billinge Hill.

Also over these next few pages Furner recalls the shock he got after giving Terry O'Connor a mouthful for being lazy in defence only to discover the big prop-forward had, for once, been seriously injured and the reasons why he had to leave the club after just two seasons.

Wigan Warriors 21 v St Helens 12

Chellenge Cup final
Saturday 27 April 2002

Murrayfield Stadium, Edinburgh
Attendance 62,140

Teams

Kris Radlinski	1	Paul Wellens
Brett Dallas	2	Darren Albertr
Gary Connolly	3	Martin Gleeson
Jamie Ainscough	4	Paul Newlove
Paul Johnson	5	Anthony Stewart
Julian O'Neill	6	Tommy Martyn
Adrian Lam	7	Sean Long
Terry O'Connor	8	Darren Britt
Terry Newton	9	Kieron Cunningham
Craig Smith	10	Peter Shiels
Mick Cassidy	11	Chris Joynt
David Furner	12	Tim Jonkers
Andy Farrell	13	Paul Sculthorpe
Substitutes		
Ricky Bibey	14	John Stankevitch
David Hodgson	15	Sean Hoppe
Mark Smith	16	Barry Ward
Brian Carney	17	Micky Higham
Newton 2, Tickle, Briscoe	**Tries**	Albert, Gleeson, Sculthorpe
Farrell 4	**Goals**	

Referee: S Cummings

MY DESIRE to come and play in the English Super League was due to having spent time in the United Kingdom in 1994 with the touring Kangaroos Australia side. I enjoyed the atmosphere at the games and the crowds were phenomenal, so I then thought that was something I would like to experience on a week-to-week basis with an English club. Towards the end of 2000 I was in a position with the Canberra Raiders, who I had played 10 seasons with, to make a decision on the future of my playing career. I then started to receive a lot of interest from English clubs. I was still playing State of Origin at the time, but I was ready for the next challenge in my career.

I was fortunate to have experienced a Grand Final with the Raiders and, along with State of Origin and Test football, I had a desire to be a part of further success and to achieve that playing in England was the next goal. I don't know if it was an omen, but when my father Don, who coached the touring Kangaroo side in 1986, came back from the tour he brought me a Wigan jersey. After looking through the offers that were on the table from Super League clubs and the playing personnel at the club at the time Wigan had the prestige that interested me and after speaking to Maurice Lindsay and "Uncle" Frank Endacott I decided that they were the club with which I could aim to achieve my next set of career goals.

LOOKING BACK I could name many a game as memorable while playing at Wigan. There was my first game for the Warriors, the Grand Final loss to Bradford in 2001 and Terry O'Connor having his nose rearranged against St Helens, but I would have to say without a doubt the Challenge Cup final against St Helens at Murrayfield in 2002 was an unforgettable experience and it was exactly what I had hoped for when I came over from Australia to play for Wigan.

The build up to that game was nerve wracking as I had not played for five weeks due to a knee injury. The Challenge Cup carries so much prestige in Australia due to its history and to be a part of one is something that I will always treasure. The game itself, being Wigan versus arch-rivals St Helens, made for even more of a special occasion. Leading up to the game there were also doubts over our full-back Kris Radlinski as he had spent time in hospital due to an infection in his foot and was having treatment to hopefully be right to play.

We stayed on the outskirts of Edinburgh for the team build-up and preparation. The feeling amongst us was confident but not cocky. We all knew we had a job to do. On the day of the game, before we boarded the bus to Murrayfield, we had a team meeting with players asked to stand up and speak about what the game meant to them and what they were going to bring to it. It's a feeling that only the players could experience, but I knew then that we were going home to Wigan with the Challenge Cup.

Arriving at Murrayfield and witnessing Super League supporters en masse in every club's colours was amazing. It was a day about rugby league and the tradition of the Challenge Cup. Every club was represented on the day, not just Wigan and St Helens, those fans were there to watch rugby league at its best.

Our coach at the time Stuart Raper had prepared us and the dressing room had that air of confidence about it before a big game and everyone from the staff to the players had a job to do. Finding out that Kris Radlinski was fit to play just added to the confidence in the players that today was going to be something special. As for my knee injury, a little help from a needle made me confident of doing a job for the team.

THE FEELING when taking that walk out onto the field lead by my life-long friend and captain Andy Farrell and the fans' roar was everything I had dreamt of. It made me realise this is the reason why we play the game for this very feeling and being in this moment.

The game was a typical Wigan versus Saints game – fast and furious and end-to-end footy. I remember receiving a nice inside ball off Faz and putting Adrian Lam in for a try. I think that was our second try of the game because fellow Australian Brett Dallas raced away to open the scoring after 11 minutes after great work from Radlinski. At one stage we were 12-0 up and we felt really good, but two quick tries from St Helens' Darren Albert and Martin Gleeson pegged us back a little and we went in leading just 12-8 at half-time.

We extended our advantage shortly after the interval when centre and former St Helens favourite Gary Connolly collected a neat pass from Paul Johnson after a fine break from Julian O'Neill to outpace the Saints defence and touch down in front of our fantastic traveling fans. We went a little crazy then and allowed Paul Sculthorpe to pull a try back, but an Adrian Lam drop-goal and an Andrew Farrell penalty sealed the victory to send everyone totally delirious. Although St Helens were a team with plenty of fire power, the feeling on the field was that we were always in control. When the final whistle went we were victorious and, looking around at the team celebrating, I couldn't help but think "how good is this?" You wouldn't want to be anywhere else at this moment.

KRIS RADLINSKI was the recipient of the Lance Todd trophy and deservedly so. As I said earlier he was a major doubt before the game because of a foot injury. If any of you had the misfortune to see the video of our doctor working on the infection you will know how much pain he was in, but when he went out on the field he was marvellous. I remember him pulling off a number of world class try-saving tackles, which looking back were probably match-saving tackles. There was one incident during the first-half which just epitomised his courage; he managed to put his body on the line and prevented Kieron Cunningham from scoring a crucial try by putting his foot under the ball to stop him from touching down. Kris deserved the Man-of-the-Match award.

Doing the lap of honour with my two children Maddison and Kyle in their Wigan jerseys was fantastic and the support of my family and friends who were there was so wonderful – they are just fantastic memories that will last forever.

Celebrations lasted well into the wee small hours and with Mick Cassidy bringing a set of clippers with him there were a few rough heads! The legendary Gary Connolly getting a hold of the microphone at the post match dinner and asking David Whelan for a bonus as only he would also brought a laugh; the night was a buzz.

On our return to Wigan we took an open topped bus through the streets to the Town Hall. That was amazing. Just seeing a sea of cherry and white jumpers and hearing the cheers and roars of the supporters was sensational. Wigan truly is a town that loves its rugby league.

MY TIME at Wigan was fantastic. We arrived with our two eldest children, who at the time were three and nearly seven. We had left Australia with temperatures of 35 degrees and landed at Manchester Airport to a cover of snow and temperatures around two or three degrees!!!!!!!!!!!!!! Welcome to the UK.

We were so pleasantly surprised at how well we settled into life in a small English village. We were living at the time in Eccleston just outside of Wigan for a short time whilst John Mawdelsey, a builder and loyal Wigan supporter, finished building a beautiful home in Heskin for our family to live in. It was truly a lovely home which we were so grateful to have been offered. Our family thrived there and we still talk about "Our Heskin House" fondly.

I instantly fitted in with the Wigan lads and some are friends that I will have for life. Maddison and Kyle, my eldest daughter and my son, were soon adapting to life in Lancashire and, before we knew it, they were asking for "crisps and sweeties" as opposed to "chips and lollies" as well as developing their own northern accents! Our youngest child Isabella was born during my time at Wigan and is known as our English Rose/Pommy Whinger depending on her mood. She is fortunate to have Andrew and Colleen Farrell as her godparents as well as being doted on by a lot of wonderful people who are special to our family.

We received a lot of support during that time from our friends which will always be appreciated. I do recall, being a long way from home, that the best form of communication with Australia was email. We had never had a computer before, so I asked our club masseur and man in the know Pinky where I could get one. He put me on to a bloke who is now a life long friend who runs Abtec Computers. Barry and his wife Denise along with their two boys Andrew and David and turned into our travel buddies. I can always recall my first meeting with Baz; his first question was "Are you going to be a dud like Greg Florimo?" No disrespect to Greg, but my reply was "I have come here to play" and I think I can say that they probably were there to watch and support me in nearly every game I did play.

No story would be complete without a mention of my mate Terry O'Connor. I can recall a game against St Helens, which of course, is the big local derby. Terry had a habit of being slow to get back in the defensive line. After making a tackle he was particularly slow getting up off the ground. I called him everything to get him back in the line! Then on one occasion he was really slow to get up after a tackle and I had a right go at him. The air was blue for the things I was calling him until he turned to face me and all I could see was his nose spread from one side of his face to the other! My response was one of shock. I then said to him "Stay down mate! Stay down! I think your modeling career is over!!"

I formed a strong bond with Andy Farrell, Denis Betts and Terry O'Connor. We were the older heads at the time and found ourselves christened "The Coffee Club" by Kris Radlinski. A special mention has to go to the Crooked Wheel, which was Terry Newton's favourite pub and many a good day and night was had there, led by non other than former Great Britain and Wigan winger Brian Carney. We had a great bond amongst the players and not to forget the backroom staff led by George the kit man!

My wife Kellie and I can truly say we loved our time overseas, obviously there were tough times with being away from family and friends and being out of your comfort zone, but we can say it was one of the best decisions we could ever have made as a family. As far as my football went, it was absolutely the best decision for me professionally. I was made welcome by the lads immediately and formed some great friendships and have many more stories to tell to friends.

My decision to leave Wigan was a bittersweet one. I had arrived on a two-year contract and honestly at the time of signing thought that would see me through to finishing up my playing career. But I underestimated how my body would hold up and how strong the desire to continue playing would be. When my contract was up for negotiation the situation was that I wanted to stay on, but due to salary cap restrictions the club was unable to keep me on the playing staff. I have to say that at the time Maurice Lindsay, who I hold in high regard, was probably as disappointed as I was that we could not make it work. I let him know that I would be looking to stay in the Super League and he wished me well as long as I did not sign with their arch rivals! I am sure that you can guess what team that is!!!!

I still keep in contact with Maurice and had a hand in getting scrum-half Michael Dobson, who is a young player with the Canberra Raiders, a season with Wigan. We touch base every so often and I have a great deal of respect for the way he does business and his devotion to the Wigan club and its players. Both Gary Connolly and myself then signed for Leeds and shared the driving down the M62 every day to training.

My first game against Wigan for Leeds was at Headingley. It was a strange feeling for me as I had only played for the one club in the NRL, so had never experienced coming up against my old team or old team-mates. It was a funny build up as I had a lot to say in team meetings about how those players played. I was well up for the game and looking forward to getting bragging rights over my old team-mates.

The game was an extremely physical one as Wigan and Leeds games are. But I will definitely remember taking a run off a tap restart and the ground being a bit dewy, putting a side step on Paul Johnson leading to me slipping a touch and PJ, who was renowned for being a big hitter, put one right on my nose with his forearm. As a result I have a permanent reminder of playing against my old side. I got up quickly and played the ball so as not to let him know he had broken it – which was hard to disguise with the blood pouring out of it. The game had a fitting end, resulting in a draw. Even with a broken nose almost everything was left out on the field except for the incident with PJ. I sure looked forward to the next battle and to get all-square. I still regard PJ as a good mate.

I still enjoy watching both clubs which I played for in England's games on Fox and watching with great interest the players I played with. My wife and I still reflect on the great times that we experienced over there and my hair still stands up on the back of my neck when the fans sing and cheer for their team. I can feel it, even though I'm thousands of miles away in Australia.

I feel so privileged to have been a part of such a wonderful experience and truly want to thank the players I have played with and the supporters of English rugby league for giving my family and me a time in our lives we will never forget and will forever reflect on with affection.

SEAN O'LOUGHLIN

LOOSE FORWARD 2002–PRESENT

SIGNED   As a 16 year-old and made his way through the academy
ranks

DEBUT   5 April 2002 versus Hull FC

WIGAN CAREER   136 appearances, 34 tries*

HONOURS   Nothing in the first team as yet

*up to and including February 2007

SEAN O'LOUGHLIN will always play rugby league with a bit of a burden on his back – no matter what he achieves he will always be linked with his brother-in-law Andrew Farrell. But he has not let it affect him; he plays the game at full-speed and is one of the best defenders in Super League. It will only be a matter of time before he is a regular in the Great Britain starting XIII challenging for honours against Australia and New Zealand.

It was difficult for Sean to cement a place in the first team when he broke through from the under 21s because no-one knew what position was his best. At such a young age he was never going to oust Andy Farrell from the loose forward role, so he started many games on the bench, or at stand-off and even centre, but he could never hold down his spot. During Farrell's last season at the club O'Loughlin was used more as a loose forward while Farrell himself was used as a prop forward. Since Farrell's departure to rugby union, O'Loughlin has taken over both the number 13 shirt and the captaincy from his brother-in-law and has revelled in the role.

O'Loughlin has his critics about his style of captaincy and his tendency to tackle above the shoulder, and some fans can beheard saying "He is no Andy Farrell", but that is O'Loughlin's point – he is not Farrell and never will be. He is Sean O'Loughlin and he goes out there every week to represent his home town club to the best of his ability.

CURRENT WIGAN skipper Sean O'Loughlin actually hopes he still has a new chapter to write regarding his best ever game in the famous cherry and white shirt, but for the moment he describes the feeling of beating a full-strength St Helens outfit on a baking hot Good Friday afternoon at the JJB Stadium when his unfancied Warriors upset the form books by defeating their arch-enemy with a team full of youngsters.

Alongside this shock victory over St Helens, one memory that will remain in O'Loughlin's mind is the day he finally got to represent his country in a first-class international test match. He appeared as a substitute for the Lions as they beat Australia in front of his own supporters at the JJB Stadium to book a place in the 2004 Tri Nations final.

On the other side of the coin, O'Loughlin shares with us the moment he knew his season was over following a horrific knee injury in 2005 and how he managed to stay sane during his long hard journey back to fitness.

Wigan Warriors 24 v St Helens 22

Super League Eight, round 6
Friday 17 April 2003

JJB Stadium
Attendance 15,607

Teams

Shaun Briscoe	1	Paul Wellens
Brian Carney	2	Ade Gardner
Martin Aspinwall	3	Martin Gleeson
Paul Johnson	4	Darren Smith
Jon Whittle	5	Darren Albert
Sean O'Loughlin	6	Paul Sculthorpe
Adrian Lam	7	Sean Long
Terry O'Connor	8	Darren Britt
Terry Newton	9	Micky Higham
Craig Smith	10	Barry Ward
Ricky Bibey	11	Chris Joynt
Danny Tickle	12	John Stankevitch
Mark Smith	13	Jason Hooper
	Substitutes	
David Allen	14	Mark Edmondson
Kevin Brown	15	Stuart Jones
Mark Roberts	16	Tim Jonkers
Danny Sculthorpe	17	Anthony Stewart
Newton 2, Tickle, Briscoe	**Tries**	Albert 2, Higham Hooper
Tickle 4	**Goals**	Sculthorpe 3

Referee: K Kirkpatrick

133

IT IS extremely hard to pick out one game for Wigan to be honest with you, but since I started playing in the first team I've always enjoyed the Good Friday games between ourselves and St Helens. They are always massive games, not just for the fans but the players as well. It is very strange because they always seem to be played in very good weather with the sun shining and the pitch is very dry.

I particularly remember one of the times when we played them back in 2003 at the JJB Stadium. It was a very tough time for us as we were struggling with a lot of injuries and a lot of younger players had been drafted into the side, but against all odds we defeated a full-strength St Helens side.

Looking back now it made it even better that we won the game because we were massive underdogs heading into the match. Basically everyone in rugby league had written us off and given us no chance of causing an upset against St Helens. We were missing a lot of first team players that day and it was an uphill struggle because they had a team full of quality stars and internationals. A mate of mine, Jon Whittle, who was playing at Orrell rugby union club at the time, got drafted in to make his Wigan debut on the wing in such an important fixture. Also Mark Roberts, another friend of mine, got his chance of first-team action after being promoted from the under 21s to have a chance to shine on the big stage.

I remember the build-up to the game because in training we were really shy of numbers and new lads and new faces were coming in from the under 21s, who had not had much involvement when it came to the first team. It was actually a bit of an uncomfortable week really because we did not want to be on the end of a real hiding or anything like that. It was just really strange being so weakened and, with so many young lads coming in, you honestly did not know how they would go on; whether they would freeze or whether they would prove that they could adapt to the situation very quickly.

The lads coming into the first team were of a similar age to myself, but had only had experience in the under 21, but they were all Wigan lads and it was a massive game for them to get thrown into the deep end against a team like St Helens, especially on a Good Friday in front of a massive crowd. I am being totally honest here when I say it really is one of the best games you could have to make an appearance in the first team – if you can't build yourself up for a game against our biggest rivals then you will never be ready.

THE GAME itself is a bit of a blur because the pace of the game was so intense. I remember Jon Whittle was having bit of a tough time marking St Helens' Australian winger Darren Albert, who got the opening the try after great work from Sean Long and Paul Sculthorpe. Albert grabbed his second try of the afternoon when Whittle failed to hold a towering bomb from Sculthorpe. We did hit back with a try from hooker Terry Newton and a great score from Danny Tickle, but tries from Mickey Higham, who is now the hooker at Wigan, and former St George Illawarra star Jason Hooper saw them lead 22-12 at half-time.

I think a lot of people thought our heads would drop after the break with such a young side and that Saints would turn us over quite convincingly, but we all dug deep and were determined to not to embarrass ourselves and the name of the club. Not long after half time Adrian Lam, who was fantastic that day, sent Mark Smith through a gap to send Shaun Briscoe over for a try and that gave us so much confidence. We never gave up and Terry Newton forced himself over from a few yards, which gave us the lead after Danny Tickle had converted. It was unbelievable; we managed to hang on at the end and I kind of remember Briscoe making a superb tackle on Darren Albert to deny him his hat-trick and prevent Saints from snatching a late victory. We hung on and everyone in that team deserved the plaudits because no-one had given us a chance all week.

The crowds for Wigan games are fantastic at any time nowadays, but when it is Wigan versus St Helens you can times the noise level by five. You can honestly not hear a thing – when you are trying to pass a message on to someone near to you on the field you have to really shout, you cannot just speak to them like normal, you have to wave your hands to get their attention and make eye contact before you can actually talk to them because it is so loud.

In a week building up to any game against St Helens you start to get the buzz because you know there is something special about the whole occasion. In my opinion, and I know there are other local derbies, I reckon Wigan verses St Helens games are the biggest ones in Super League. I know there has been a lot of talk about us playing them four times during the 2007 season, I do not think it is fair to be playing any side four times really – I think it should be split up and we play every team the same number of times. Don't get me wrong, I know it is not always possible to arrange it that way, but in previous seasons we have sometimes played teams three times, but never on four occasions.

I have been lucky enough to have played in a couple of victories over them, but one of my worst memories in the game also happened in a Good Friday clash against St Helens. It was in 2005 when we faced them at the JJB Stadium and I sustained my serious knee injury. I think that was around the 7th game of the season when I actually did my knee, and as soon as I went into the tackle I knew I had done something really bad. I then had to have a scan and see a specialist and things like that, but straight away I had ruled myself out for the rest of the season. There was no chance of me playing towards the back end of the season – that would have been way too early. It kind of made it a little bit easier because there was no rush to get me back on the field, no specific timescale set or anything like that. I knew that I would be starting back for pre-season training with everyone else so I just focused on that really. There was never any case of me rushing and pushing myself to get just one game under my belt because I knew deep down I needed to return fully fit.

It was a very tough to be sat on the sidelines, but, on the other hand, in the same season, Gareth Hock had done his knee just two weeks before mine and around a week or two later Paul Prescott also did his knee. So there was three of us there doing all our training together and that makes it a little bit easier. Anyone who has been injured will probably tell you that the worst thing about it is training on your own – you cannot train with the team because they are out on the field. You can do your weights and that kind of thing, but a lot of the time you're just on your own. We were lucky.

There was a little group of us. It was quite tough watching the team from the back of the stand, twitching about on your seat trying to help, so yeah I did get a bit frustrated watching, especially that season because we were doing it tough and we struggled a lot. When the team is not doing well you just want to be out there helping them, not necessarily thinking "oh we would have won if I'd have played" nothing like that – you just want to be part of the team.

So that was really tough on myself and the team, but then I was handed the captaincy. To be named captain of Wigan I can honestly say was the greatest thing. I was absolutely made up. It was a massive honour for me, with me being from Wigan. And as I used to watch them as a kid at Central Park it made the honour more special for me.

I was actually still out injured at the time and Basil [Ian Millward], who was coach of Wigan at the time, told me with a few weeks to go in the season that I would be the new captain at the start of the next season. When it was announced it was a great occasion – in fact it was actually announced around the time I got married . It was a busy couple of weeks for us. I think I got named captain at the beginning of the week and got married at the end of the week, something like that, so I was on a bit of a high to be honest with you.

I'D SIGNED for the club when I was 16 years old. I did my apprentice-ship in the Academy and the under 21s. At that time we had a lot of older fringe first-teamers playing for us as well. Now it is basically all under 21s, but when I played you did have some first-team players around you and you did get to know them quite well.

I was 19 years-old when I signed a full-time contract at Wigan. There were a lot of senior players in the squad at that time like Andy Farrell, Kris Radlinski, Terry O'Connor and Mick Cassidy. I think it was the same year that Craig Smith came over as well, so there was a lot of big-name players in the squad. They all had an aura about them and it was quite daunting to be honest. I knew Andy Farrell beforehand from family as he was my brother-in-law, so that wasn't as daunting as it was to meet the other senior players. At the same time Luke Robinson came up with me from the under 21s, as did Stephen Wild, so I did have some of my mates with me at the time which meant an awful lot.

I know a lot of people make a big deal about Andy Farrell being my brother-in-law and are always making comparisons. It is something I do get a lot of the time – not necessarily comparisons, but people always mention about following in his footsteps. I just look at it as a compliment; if I am being compared to someone like Faz, probably one of the best players in rugby league when he was here, then I'm a happy man. At the end of the day if I'm being compared to him I must be doing something right in my career.

THAT victory over Saints was probably the best game I have ever played myself, and is probably the best game I've ever been involved in for Wigan. But my first Great Britain match, when we beat Australia at the JJB Stadium, was also very special.

It was in the Tri-Nations series in 2005. I was supposed to be playing in one of the games a few weeks before that match, but I ended up missing it because I was ill. I also did not get picked the following week. So one week it looked like I was going to make my debut, but then I had to wait another two weeks.

I was on the bench for the game. Looking back it was probably a big game for me because it was at the JJB Stadium in front of near enough a sell-out crowd. It was just an ambition of mine to play for Great Britain and I ended up making my debut on my home ground, which made it even more special. Plus the added bonus at the end was that we won the game. That was my first Test jersey and my first cap – you get to keep your jersey after the game and I've still got it. In fact I got it signed after the game and it is now framed and up on my wall.

It's not that I thought I had a great game or anything like that, but the occasion was fantastic. That feeling when you get handed your first Great Britain jersey is something you will always treasure. It's a special, special feeling. Also victory over Australia ended a run of seven straight defeats against the Kangaroos, I think. It also sealed our place in the first final of the Tri Series tournament which was a special moment for me. Unfortunately we did not back that performance up in the final a couple of weeks later and got heavily beaten.

From what I can remember sitting on the bench, the Aussies took the lead with a try from Luke Rooney, who collected a kick from Brett Kimorley. After a strong opening period it looked like the Aussies would take control, but we dug deep and started to hit back. Terry Newton pounced on a loose ball to score, before more quick tries from Stuart Reardon, who took advantage of fantastic play from Farrell, and Stuart Fielden, who crossed for his first ever try for his country took us from being 6-0 down to 18-6 up, with 25,000 vocal fans right behind us.

Our defence in the second half was nothing short of superb, they did cross for an early try through prop forward Mark O'Meely, but, despite their constant pressure, everyone one of us from one to 17 played their part in a marvellous performance. The icing on the cake came when Keith Senior picked up on a loose ball to race 60 yards to seal a memorable win over the old enemy. I will always treasure that 24-12 victory, it is just a shame it came to nothing in the final.

LOOKING BACK at the players I have played with I've been lucky to play alongside some great ones – Kris Radlinski, Andy Farrell and Terry O'Connor were all fantastic players, but they set an example off the field as well in the way they spoke to you. They did their extras and worked hard, whether they were injured or not. Those types of players are the kind you try and model yourself on with their attitude and the way they conduct themselves.

There is not one player during my career I actually feared, but one of the best players I actually played against was Darren Lockyer. I only played against him a few times and he has probably been the difference between the two sides each time. He's been doing it for over 10 years and he seems to be getting better and better. He moved from full-back to stand-off and he's just an awesome player. He has to be the best I've come up against; he bosses the game even without touching the ball sometimes. He can just control a game and make things happen.

Being at Wigan is great at the moment, for the 2007 season we signed Trent Barrett and Shane Millard which brought senior heads to the squad because we have had quite a younger set up in previous years. Those players have not just taken some pressure off me as a captain, I like to have people around me like Baz, (Trent Barrett), Fletcher (Bryan Fletcher), and Billy (Shane Millard). They add a bit of experience to the lads. When I was coming through we had Andy Farrell, Terry O'Connor and Mick Cassidy – they all helped the young lads come through and we have got a bit of a similar thing happening now. There could be great times ahead for Wigan.

KEVIN BROWN

CENTRE/STAND-OFF 2003–2006

SIGNED Signed from Thatto Heath amateur club and made his way up through the academy ranks

DEBUT 17 April 2003 versus St Helens

WIGAN CAREER 73 appearances, 31 tries

HONOURS Challenge Cup runner-up 2004

LEFT For a loan spell at Huddersfield Giants near the end of the 2006 season, before signing a permanent deal

KEVIN BROWN emerged on the Super League scene at the tender age of 18 when Wigan faced arch-rivals St Helens. Wigan were undergoing a very serious injury crisis and had to call upon youngsters such as Kevin Brown, Shaun Briscoe, David Allen, Jon Whittle and Mark Roberts to even field a side.

Brown was victorious on his debut and Sky Sports commentator Mike Stephenson was so impressed with his performance that he purchased him a watch normally given to the Man-of-the-Match winner, because he felt he handled himself under intense pressure.

Unfortunately, and Kevin admits to this, he never lived up to the expectations Wigan supporters had of him; some expected him to become a world-beater overnight. When Ian Millward came in as the coach, instead of guiding the youngster through a difficult time, he continued to heap pressure on him by talking him up as the next Great Britain stand-off. This ended up being too much for such a young lad and the Wigan faithful began to get on his back.

Despite always giving everything in a Wigan shirt, Brown has now resurrected his career over in Yorkshire with Huddersfield and has started to find his form he had when he first broke into the Wigan squad. In a Super League clash in April 2007 at the Galpharm Stadium, Brown was part of the Giants side that comprehensively defeated Wigan 41-16.

IN 2003 Wigan went through a major injury crisis which saw them having to promote quite a few youngsters to the first team well ahead of schedule. Kevin Brown was one of them and he admits to having two favourite games during his few years with Wigan and they both involved victories against arch-rivals St Helens.

During this chapter Brown talks about the strange feeling he got when warming up to see so many familiar faces in the crowd and also the shock he received when celebrating a try at Knowsley Road to see a former school friend stood in a Saints shirt glaring right back at him.

Brown also reveals the hurt and disappointment he felt after becoming a scapegoat the 2006 season in which Wigan suffered a terrible campaign and narrowly avoided relegation with only a few weeks remaining. Brown also reveals the debt of gratitude he owes to former coach Mike Gregory, who had to give up his career because of illness, for the guidance he gave while in charge at the JJB Stadium. Brown honestly declares he would have gone out on the pitch to die for Gregory.

St Helens 34 v Wigan Warriors 38

Super League Eight, round 13
Friday 6 June 2003

Knowsley Road
Attendance 12,837

Teams

Paul Wellens	1	Shaun Briscoe
Anthony Stewart	2	Paul Johnson
Paul Newlove	3	Martin Aspinwall
Martin Gleeson	4	Kevin Brown
Ade Gardner	5	David Hodgson
Paul Sculthorpe	6	Sean O'Loughlin
Sean Long	7	Adrian Lam
Darren Britt	8	Craig Smith
Kieron Cunningham	9	Terry Newton
Keith Mason	10	Terry O'Connor
Mike Bennett	11	Mick Cassidy
Chris Joynt	12	Nathan Graham
Darren Smith	13	Andy Farrell
	Substitutes	
Jason Hooper	14	Mark Smith
Micky Higham	15	Danny Sculthorpe
Barry Ward	16	Gareth Hock
Stuart Jones	17	Luke Robinson

Gleeson, Wellens, Ward, Gardner, Smith 2	**Tries**	Robinson 3, Brown 2, Hodgson
Sculthorpe 5	**Goals**	Farrell 7

Referee: R Smith

ONE OF my most memorable games in a Wigan shirt was when we played St Helens at Knowsley Road in 2003. I think we were about 20 points down at one stage, but stunned everyone to hit back and claim a fantastic win.

We had a weakened side and the build up to the game was hard. The Saints team in front of us had a number of internationals in it; facing us were players like Chris Joynt and Martin Gleeson. I remember speaking to Luke Robinson before the game and he was really nervous. It was great that I ended up scoring two tries, while Luke crossed for his hat-trick. He also got Man of the Match. I was over the moon for him. I remember watching it back on TV a while after the game and everyone associated with Wigan was going mad at the final whistle. You could see the chairman Maurice Lindsay jumping up and down like the rest of our supporters and Stuart Raper, the coach at the time, was trying to calm him down.

As MOST people would know I am from the St Helens area being from Haydock and I was nervous during the build up to playing my first game at Knowsley Road, I had played the Saints at home and we won. You don't really think anything like that can happen. Saints were really going well in the league and we had a bit of an under-strength team with a lot of experience unavailable for selection. We couldn't believe our luck the first time we'd beat them on Good Friday at Wigan, but to beat them at their place was beyond the realms of believability. I remember standing on the pitch before the game and people who I knew from the area were shouting for me and I was looking around feeling dead nervous. Once the game starts, though, you get caught up in the drama and you are focused. The game itself went dead quick, it seemed like it was over after only five minutes.

Once I found out I was playing I had everyone asking me whether I was nervous, asking me by how many points Saints would beat us, if they would batter us and things like that. I received hundreds of text messages and jokes from my mates giving it loads. As a player all you want to do really is play well, but when you are that nervous you just try to ignore the other things that are going on. I remember when I scored one of my tries I jumped up near to the crowd and I saw one of the girls I'd been to school with and she had a Saints top on. It was just a really weird feeling; not long before that I had been a child growing up on the terraces at Wigan. It didn't seem long ago that it was me stood on the popular side at Central Park like those fans and here I am playing for my boyhood team against the local enemy.

It was a mad feeling after going to watch Wigan as a young lad and going through all the emotions imaginable throughout a season as a fan and then here I was going through different emotions a few years later playing for them.

We were 20 nil down and I'm just thinking, "oh my god, we are going to get hammered here." Then as soon as you get on the score sheet, the fans start cheering and then you start gaining confidence thinking, "we could score again ." We then scored one try and then another and then another. We just kept going and ended up winning the game. Emotionally it was one of the best feelings aside from my debut earlier in the season.

M Y DEBUT was unreal. We were missing around five first teamers as the injury crisis bit for the first time that season. We had Jon Whittle on the wing, Mark Roberts was playing, Dave Allen played as well, as did Shaun Briscoe. We had a very young side, but we still had great players with experience. Adrian Lam was still out there, as was Terry Newton and I remember in the build up to the game Julian O'Neill was winding me up saying that that I was crapping my pants. He even put a toilet roll on my peg in the dressing room. I didn't know he'd done it and all the lads were laughing at me. I'm stood there thinking, "what are they all doing laughing? We are going out in a bit." Then I realised after he had put toilet roll above my head. When we went out I was looking around at their team and they were massive compared to us. They had all their senior players playing, the likes of Paul Sculthorpe, Sean Long and

Kieron Cunningham. We had Jon Whittle and myself, though Luke Robinson was out injured. Mark Smith was playing loose. This was just like the team I'd played in for the academy, so to go out and stick with them was fantastic.

We were obviously fitter than them as we were smaller, but no-one expected us to win and at the end we were like, "have we won this? We can't have won this game". We eventually got back into the changing rooms. I think we were out on the pitch for about 10 minutes after the game had ended still cheering. I couldn't believe that feeling. I remember Dean Bell saying, "you will only get one better feeling than this and that is winning the Cup – that will be the best feeling you'll ever have."

During that game on Sky TV the commentator and former Great Britain hooker Mike 'Stevo' Stephenson was waxing lyrical about my performance and afterwards he even bought me the same watch that the Man of the Match gets as he believed I should have won it and I didn't. I think that did put a bit of pressure on me when news of it got out. I wanted to go out each week and get that feeling again, but it never panned out like that unfortunately. I had some good games and we went to Cardiff for the Challenge Cup Final but we got beat. Obviously I was a bit down after that. I had a lot of expectations after my debut; a couple of weeks later I scored my first hat trick against Halifax and I think I set myself really high standards to live up to. When I started to have a few poor games the fans started to get on my back and I think as a really young lad it hurt because when I was a fan I thought the players who used to get slagged off were not really trying. But I was trying even harder to play well when my form dipped. I think that was because I was trying too hard and when the fans continued to get on my back I had no confidence.

It seemed I had become a sort of scapegoat because Wigan were not playing well and for me it was one of the worst feelings I've ever had. I was a Wigan lad through and through – in the end it kind of left me with a bitter feeling because people didn't like me. I didn't feel like I had done anything wrong. All I had done was try my best. People were saying things like I wasn't trying for the team and that I was taking drugs. I was getting phone calls saying you are this and you've been seen doing this, I've heard from this from someone else, so it must be true. In the end I just had to stop listening as it was making me so down.

I honestly felt I needed to leave the club. I could have come back for the 2007 season, but I got my form back at Huddersfield and started playing well again. Brian Noble and Maurice Lindsay both wanted me back, but I just thought I needed the change. I was really enjoying my rugby again and I was playing better for it – that is the main thing. If you are enjoying what you do you feel so much better about yourself. I just wasn't enjoying playing rugby at the end of my time at Wigan because of all the pressure of relegation fight and the personal pressures. A lot of people say you should not listen to things like that, but it is hard not to listen when they are being said about you.

It is hard, you know. I'm still only 22 now, so it was definitely hard as I was getting used to getting praised and then it all changed with everyone saying, "he's crap and Wigan should just get rid of him, he's no good for the team," and things like that. It was honestly like a stake through my heart and I just thought I had to get out and start concentrating on my rugby and I have started doing that now and just hope I can carry this on.

When he was coach at Wigan Ian Millward put a lot of pressure on my shoulders. You had some fans saying I wasn't good enough to play for Wigan and then Ian was telling everyone that I was going to be the future of Great Britain Rugby League. I don't think that helped me. Once again it just put a lot of pressure on me and I think I was just trying too hard. I wanted to be Man of the Match week in week out and I set my expectations too high. Once I had a few bad games it sort of snowballed from there really. It was honestly the worst feeling you could ever have. Being a fan myself when you hear your own fans turning against you, you start thinking maybe its time to move on.

ANOTHER FANTASTIC moment in my career was playing the Challenge Cup Final at the Millennium Stadium in Cardiff against St Helens in 2004. I know we lost, but it was still one of my best moments. I had a coach there that I would have died for in Mike Gregory. He is one of the best people in the world. I have so much respect for him and I still go and see him now. It's a shame about his health now, but when he was coach at Wigan. He did nothing but help me. He put his arm around me when I wasn't playing so well and congratulated me when I was playing well. I think that is what I really needed from a coach at that time. He looked after me and didn't let me get big-headed or anything like that. It was an honour to play for him in that cup final, which happened to be his last. I thought a win would have been the perfect way to thank him for what he did for me, but we lost. I honestly thought we had the team that could have won that game. We had a few tries disallowed. I don't like making excuses, but looking back I still think there were some certain tries that day like that one of mine – I could not see a knock on. Then after that Andy Farrell also had one chalked off, so it could have been a whole different ball game.

To beat Saints in a cup final would have been a dream come true and to be honest it was what I expected because we had beaten Saints that many times in recent years. I expected to beat them. We had beaten them with weak sides with loads of youngsters in. For this game we had players like Andy Farrell, Adrian Lam and Terry Newton. We had class all over the park in the likes of Quentin Pongia and Craig Smith. I still don't know how we did not win that game,

In the build up to it, there was such a great feeling – we had people crying in meetings saying how much it meant to them to win it for Mike Gregory. Every player wore their heart on their sleeves that day. We were just unfortunate to get beaten on the day by a good side, and you just have to hold your hands up really.

When you walk out at Cardiff, you have a singer singing and everyone is blowing their horns – the hair on the back of your neck stands up. You are looking around thinking about how many people are there. You can't believe they have all come to watch you. It goes in the blink of an eye and then the game is over and you've either won or lost and unfortunately on that occasion we lost, but it was definitely great to play there.

DURING MY time at Wigan I managed to play under a few coaches. Stuart Raper was my first coach; I think his decision to give me my first team chance was forced upon him really with the injury crisis we were going through. But Stuart was really good with me. He taught me stuff about my game. He didn't just throw me in and pull me out, he actually told me where I was going right and where I was going wrong, so he was good. I thought he was a really good coach even though I didn't get much chance to work with him because he got the sack about two months after that. Mike Gregory then took over and from that moment my career really took off. Mike gave me a chance and I kind of claimed that left centre spot. I was selected there every week – that was due to Mike giving me a chance and also me taking that chance with open arms. I played well and that was the best season I had with Wigan. Brett Dallas was the winger on the outside of me and I had Adrian Lam and Andy Farrell on my inside. It's dead easy playing well when you've got players like that giving you great passes. And defensively they knew where to be. It was a great time to be playing for the Wigan Warriors.

When Mike got too ill to continue as coach, Denis Betts took over. Denis did a great job with the team that he had. It was quite a young side and when Andy Farrell, Craig Smith and Mick Cassidy left he didn't really replace them with senior heads. We had good young players, but nothing surrounding that, so Denis in my opinion had a tough task on his hands. He did a good job and I personally don't think Maurice Lindsay gave him enough time; I think he just panicked and got rid when the going got tough.

Ian Millward was the next to come in as coach and I thought Basil would be awesome, but for me he put a lot of pressure on my shoulders. He was harsh on the young lads in training sessions and it was really hard to play well for him. When Brian Noble came in I only played one game under him. He initially asked me if I wanted to go out on loan? I said, "I love it here at Wigan and I'd rather stop here if you can give me a chance." He replied, "I don't want you to go for the rest of the year, just for four weeks." I said, "if that's all it's for then I'll go," so I was on my way to Huddersfield. Then Wigan rang me up and said, "you're playing this week, so come back," so I never made it to Huddersfield.

A week later Stuart Fielden signed for Wigan and Brian informed me that I had to leave again as the Huddersfield deal was back on; but this time the deal was until the end of the year and not just for the original four weeks as previously stated. I think one of the reasons was the salary cap, but I wasn't getting selected anyway. I was disappointed how it ended up, it never really finished the way I would have liked it too. I would love to still be playing for Wigan. I'm still a Wiganer at heart, but it's a career and we all need money, so I had to leave. I am loving my time at Huddersfield. I didn't expect it to be a professional set up to honest with you, but Jon Sharp has a great club here and it's quite similar to Wigan in some respects.

WITHOUT A doubt in my Wigan career, there are two players who were just fantastic to play with. There was Andy Farrell, who was just a freak. He was the fittest and strongest man on the pitch, but not only that he is one of the cleverest on there as well. Not many people would say he was clever, but in the video meetings he would come up with points and he would get them across to you and it would make a massive difference on game day. Some fans say now about Sean O'Loughlin not being a good captain, Andy Farrell did a lot of shouting behind the sticks but flipping heck he didn't do any shouting when he was taking the ball in and knocking people off him. That was what we all looked at. We, as his team-mates, didn't care about him shouting, no-one really takes much notice of that. It's incidents like when he came back onto the field with a broken nose and things like that, that's why we all looked up to him and aspired to be like him.

Andy Farrell was an enforcer. When he spoke to people they looked and listened. To have a player like that at the side of you is going to make a massive difference. When he was not there, or even when he had a rare off game, he still made players play better with his presence because you wanted to show him you are good enough to be on the same pitch with one of the best players in the world.

There was an incident during a Good Friday clash at Knowsley Road a few years back. Terry Newton started hitting Jon Wilkin. I tried splitting it up by pulling Sean Long away, then Don Feuanati starting choking me with his hands around my neck. Paul Sculthorpe and Mark Edmondson came in and starting punching Stephen Wild. Faz then came in and had a go at Scully basically saying, "you are just bullying them." That shows what Andy Farrell for what he was like. He was Wigan through and through and he would have died for any of us and we would have died for Faz because he was that respected at the club and I think everyone still respects him as a player and a person.

The second player who had a massive influence on my rugby league career was Adrian Lam. I learned loads off him during our time at Wigan – his ball handling skills and his quick thinking were second to none, you could tell the difference instantly when Lammy left and we signed Dennis Moran. Moran was a cracking player, he really was, but the influence Adrian Lam had over the whole team was amazing. He organised everyone. Everyone would know where they were going. He would do it every week and I suppose we all took it for granted, so when he left there was a massive void there.

Those two players for me stand out head and shoulders above everyone else.

I've spoken about the players I've played with who were fantastic to work with, but there are a couple of players who you always knew where going to give you a hard game – Paul Sculthorpe always seemed to target me and run at me. He was a handful every time we had the opportunity to face each other. When I played at centre Martin Gleeson was hard to play against. He is a nightmare to defend against because of his feet. You think he's going one way, you blink, and he's gone the other way and scored under the sticks.

PLAYING FOR Wigan was a dream come true. I couldn't have asked for anything better, I've said before about the fans giving me a bit of stick, but all fans gets frustrated. You have expectations of Wigan always being at the top and they have probably been spoiled with all the success. You could say I shouldn't have listened to the criticism that was flung at me, but I can't complain about my time at Wigan. I loved every minute of it and it's such a shame it was only for a few years. It was a privilege and an honour to play for such a great club. I would love to go back, but I think things would have to change from when I played there.

I think with Brian Noble in charge now Wigan will soon be back up there as a major force in rugby league. I am not saying they will suddenly start winning every trophy in sight but the foundations are now in place for the future and it does look good. From a personal point of view with regards to my own career I want to play for the big clubs, so I would never say I would never go back to Wigan.